FRANK Pranks

FRANK Pranks

Steve Collins and Alan Martin, eds.

The publication of *FRANK Pranks* has been generously supported by
the Canada Council, the Ontario Arts Council, and by
the Government of Canada through the Book Publishing Industry Development Program.

CANADIAN CATALOGUING IN PUBLICATION DATA

Frank pranks
ISBN 1-55022-416-6
1. Celebrities — Canada — Interviews. 2. Celebrities — Canada — Humour.
I. Collins, Steve, 1971- . II. Martin, Alan, 1970- . III. Title: Frank (Ottawa edition).
FC25.F722 2000   920.071   C00-931718-X   F1005.F722 2000

Cover Design by Sean McCool.
Interior Design by Sean McCool.
This book is set in the Franklic Gothic type family and Times New Roman.

Printed by AGMV, l'Imprimeur, Cap-Saint-Ignace, Quebec
Distributed by General Distribution Services,
325 Humber College Blvd., Etobicoke, Ontario M9W 7C3.

Published by ECW PRESS
2120 Queen Street East, Suite 200,
Toronto, Ontario M4E 1E2.
ecwpress.com

PRINTED AND BOUND IN CANADA

FRANK PRANKS   CONTENTS

This is a book. A real, honest to goodness, fancy FRANK book. Take a moment to run your tongue over the high-quality paper. Mmmmm. Smooth.

What's in it? Glad you asked, poppet. For the first time, we've collected over five years of our infamous FRANK phone pranks, wherein our operatives dial up your favourite windbag politicos, onanist showbiz types, and other deserving victims, then feed them a line and let their egos take over.

From the very beginning, FRANK Pranks revealed themselves to be a cost-effective way to get some cheap, cruel laughs at the expense of prominent Canadians and fill a couple of pages on a slow news day — they were also darned educational.

When we placed a bogus personals ad for Sheila Copps, it revealed her betrothal to the current Mr. Copps, ex-union thingy Austin Thorne. The handsome his and hers FRANK T-shirts we sent as a wedding gift were graciously returned.

At the height of the Airbus scandal, we launched a faux legal defence fund for Prime Suspect Byron Muldoon. The depth of loyalty among his supplicants was telling. Grand total pledged: $50. At least *Globe and Mail* editrix Bill Thorsell, while declining to shell out for the cause, promised not to breathe a word of the fundraising campaign to his newspaper. Loyalty still counts for something, eh?

Loopy *Law and Order* star Michael Moriarty mentioned that in his salad days he'd been confined to a mental institution and subjected to electro-shock therapy. Ovide Mercredi, Al Waxman, Elwy Yost, and (pas possible) Maggie Trudeau-Kemper had all dabbled in marijuana back in their day. Mercredi was unmoved by the $95,000 tax-free, plus perks we were offering him as

Governor-General because it would be such a cut from his current take-home as a professional Indian.

Fellow candidate Adrienne Clarkson, meanwhile, displayed a perfect command of the icy vice-regal tone, not to mention a completely non-partisan first-name familiarity with the movers and shakers of the Crouton PMO. As for our job offer, forget it; she already knew she had the sinecure in the bag.

The elements of a successfully executed prank? Use the art of misdirection to pack the prank with small absurdities, ask open ended questions and then give the sucker enough phone cord to hang himself. For example, no one looked askance the time we called various Reformers to tell them they'd been outed by the Gay Empowerment Rights Bipartisan League (GERBiL). They were too busy telling us how straight they were. We never did get the tearful confession of a closeted life in Preston's caucus, but a few did protest too much. Not that there's anything wrong with that . . .

Other helpful hints from the FRANK playbook.

Rule number one: Know your target. Stereotypical thinking will get you farther than you'd think. The latte-sucking Toronto snob in us said the Reformers would believe almost anything you told them about the mythical sushi fish. We were soooo right.

Rule number two: Tell 'em what they want to hear. Feed neo-con nutters tall tales of government profligacy and political correctness. Unwashed lefties need yarns of corporate rapacity to work themselves up into a proper lather.

Rule number three: Deny, deny, deny. If they ask if this is some kind of joke, assure them you're deadly serious. You don't read FRANK. You've never heard of FRANK. Who's FRANK?

Despite our intricate planning, pranking can be a weird ride. Note the eerie prescience of the good men and women of the psychic hotlines, who for $3.99 a minute accurately predicted that Paul Bernardo would go to the clink largely because of reptilian spouse Karla Homolka, sensed that Stan

FRANK PRANKS

Faulder's trip to Texas was definitely one-way ("Oh my God, you're going to get the needle!"), and presaged Matt Barrett's "retirement" and impending bachelorhood. Gooseflesh all 'round when in the middle of one of our spiels, one of LaToya's clairvoyants suddenly blurted out, "Are you sure you're telling me the truth?" Brrrr.

Worst moment: Calling up Robert Homme (AKA The Friendly Giant) to offer him the gig as Governor-General. Any reason you couldn't take the job, we asked? "Er, well, yes. I'm dying." Eeek. We quickly assured Friendly we'd pass that on to the PMO, terribly sorry, etc. etc. And as far as we know, the old guy kicked off believing he'd once been asked to be vice-regent. As long as that friggin' Rusty kept his beak zipped.

Sharing the award for biggest crybaby in the annals of prankdom are *National Post* editor Ken "Perry" Whyte and gasbag Muldoon crony Stu "Stu" Hendin. After being gulled by FRANK operatives (Whyte as a potential nude centrefold for *Cosmo*, Hendin as a potential donor to the Airbus defence fund) both filed fraud complaints with the cops.

Law enforcement officers who a) have a couple more pressing jobs to do, and b) know a friggin' joke when they hear one, declined to press charges.

We must also count our blessings.

The Reform/Canadian Alliance Party provided a virtually endless supply of rubes who could be relied upon to fulminate on command on the hot-button issue of our choice. Was it the democratic urge to answer their own calls or the fact that the party's awash in moronic hicks who can't resist teeing off on pinkos, homos, and fer'ners? Who cares? Thanks for the memories, Myron.

Special thanks must be also given for the bottomless gullibility of beloved film buff Elwy Yost, who was always available, always credulous and more often than not on the john ("Could you wait until I get some clothes on?"). Our punishment? The stubborn, indelible image of a naked Elwy that we will all take to the grave.

INTRODUCTION

Al Waxman's hubris never ceased to produce the desired result. No honour — from Tory candidate and potential cabinet minister to the office of Governor-General — was too great for the King of Kensington to consider it only his due. Best o' luck on that Senate seat, Al, baby!

And a moment of silence, please, for patsy extraordinaire Lorne Nystrom, who silly-walked his way into FRANK Prank history when he bought our canard about Tubby Black taking government grants for study at the prestigious Cleese Institute of Heraldry. An outraged NDP press release, official,denials and litigation followed in giddily short order.

Of course, we couldn't have perpetrated this six-year crime spree without fellow pranksters, like G.M. and his legendary deadpan, able to sell the most ludicrous scenarios with that brusque, business-like drone of a voice. Thanks also to E.H. and her shameless flirtation, used to such deadly effect when we went canvassing for *Cosmo*'s "Hunks of the North."

Before our field agents even start dialing, of course, we rely on the exquisite cunning and misanthropy of D.M. and J.W., two of Canada's most merciless satirists, who profile our victims' weaknesses and plan the attack. They script the elaborate snow jobs complete with punch-lines that invariably hit sometime after the mark hangs up.

We would also be remiss if we didn't thank our cast of Great Canadians™ for their remarkably narcissistic, artless, and oh-so-revealing performances of self-abasement. So thanks. Suckers.

(March 3, 1994)

Sheila Copps Dial-a-Date

Sheila Copps, be lonely no more. FRANK has undertaken the task of finding you a new man.

Copps has been single since 1990, when she separated from her second husband, Ric Marrero, an underemployed sound engineer and convicted drunk driver.

Sheila's previous marriage, when she was 23, lasted less than a year. Despite a series of liaisons since her break-up with Marrero, the deputy prime minister has never settled down with one special guy . . . or girl.

To remedy this situation, FRANK placed an ad in the Women Seeking Men section of the Ottawa Citizen's *"RSVP" telepersonals and recorded an outgoing message*

— in an irritating nasal timbre — on our "voice mailbox." Almost immediately after our ad appeared, "Sheila's" voice mail was deluged by responses from lonely hearts.

Our little stunt even made headlines in the Ottawa Citizen, *appearing in Jane Taber's Feb. 2 Official Circles column: "the latest in a string of jokes at Copps' expense . . . the kind of reaction, bordering on sexism, that Copps, a strong and powerful woman, provokes."*

The following are transcriptions of the most intriguing responses we received. The names and numbers have been withheld to protect identities. They will be forwarded to Sheila's office upon her request.

FRANK assessment: Might be fun for a quick fling, but age difference doesn't bode well for a long-term relationship.

• "Hello, Nobody's Baby. I believe we've already met. Does Clifford Bowie Pool, around October, ring a bell? It was in the hot tub. My name's [NAME] and my son's name is [NAME]. I'm 38 years old, separated for a year, 6' 2", 200 lbs. Ah, give me a call [NUMBER]. Ah, I may have to become a Ti-Cats fan if things don't work out here in Ottawa. Anyway, I'm open to suggestions. Hope to talk to you soon. Bye-bye."

FRANK assessment: In a hot tub? With his son? We'd rather forget the whole thing.

• "Uh, hi. This is Claude. I'm 35 years old, blue eyes, brown hair. Uh, I'm 5'8", 160. I'm considered attractive, intelligent, um, sincere. Um . . . [COUGHS] . . . Uh, what else? Um, I'm very romantic. What else? I love to play. I love to have a good time. Um, I'm also French, so how 'bout giving a French guy a chance [LAUGHS]. So if you want to give me a call, my phone number is [NUMBER]. You can reach me after 5:00 on weekdays — I do work in the daytime — and weekends anytime. So, talk to you soon. Bye-bye."

FRANK assessment: Tubercular wheezing a turn-off, but dating a francophone wouldn't hurt. Worth a try.

• "I really enjoyed your ad, it was cute. No, my name is [NAME]. I'm 34 years old, tall, long hair. Um, um, I

£917.   129269

NOBODY'S baby! Prominent, outspoken single mom, early forties, Politically active, tough as nails. Seeks Italian man (or other) for tequila and Ti-Cats. No drugs. RSVP 2949.   138415

~~NONSMOKER~~, college student, 20, 5'11, blue

• "Hi, it, uh — you sound very interesting. You sound like somebody who I think I might know of, and, um, anyway, it'd be very interesting to hear from you, uh, 'cause I admire a woman of, uh, whoever — similar to what you sound like in your ad. I'm 24 years old myself. I know that's a bit

younger, but, uh, I hope that doesn't matter. I really would like to meet you. So, uh, why don't you get back to me and give me a call some time at [NUMBER]. The best time to reach me is in the evenings after about seven o'clock. So give me a call. Bye for now."

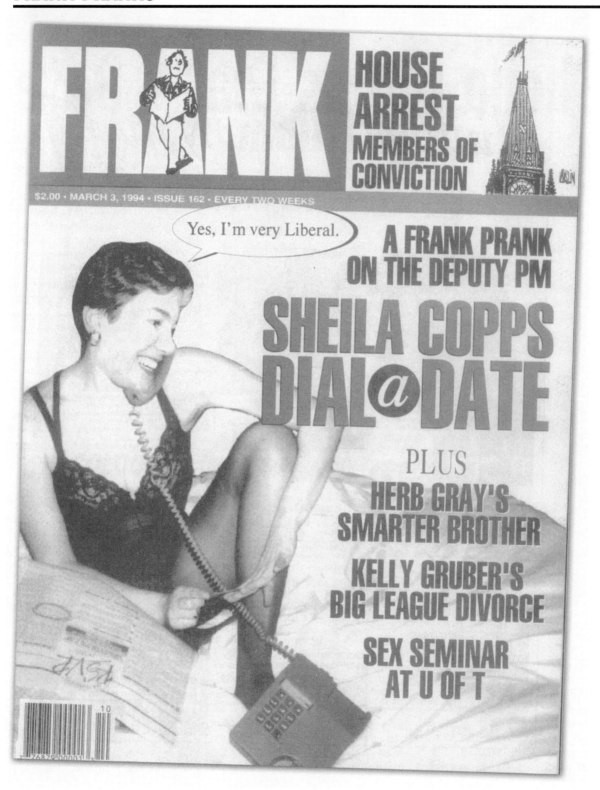

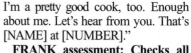

enjoy lots of things — very active. And, uh, somewhat politically so, but mostly active in sports and that kind of thing. I enjoy socializing and, uh, getting out and having fun. So, if you want to chat, why not give me a call? My number is [NUMBER]. Bye for now."

FRANK assessment: Boastful jockette. Probably lacks the graces required for the position. Next.

• "This is [NAME] at [NUMBER]. Would your initials be S.C.? If so, 'politically active' is an understatement. I've been politically aware since childhood. My father was a [TITLE OF SENIOR GOVT. OFFICIAL]. We used to get phone calls at home from the premier. I used to watch provincial Question Period for amusement. Anyway, about me. I just turned 43. I'm divorced, I have one daughter. I'm pure WASP. My mom came over as a British war bride. Although I have an I.Q. of 138 and a Bachelor of Science, I'm an underachiever. Recently I [UNINTELLIGIBLE] public service clerical positions. I don't smoke. I do take prescription drugs daily but nothing else. I like to play games, watch movies. I travel when I can afford to. I adore children and I have two cats which I baby.

I'm a pretty good cook, too. Enough about me. Let's hear from you. That's [NAME] at [NUMBER]."

FRANK assessment: Checks all the boxes, domestically, but proud confession to government job a strike against him. Bonus points for scripted and rehearsed message. The best of the lot.

• "Hi, Sheila, it's [NAME]. I have all of the aforementioned qualities on your tape with the exception of the fact that I'm not, uh, Italian. But I have Anglo-Saxon origins. Can you give me a call at [NUMBER]? Talk to you soon, *Ciao*."

FRANK assessment: Too brief a message, but Italian sign-off is a nice touch. Maybe.

• "Hi, my name is [NAME]. I'm a single professional male. I'm a businessman, running a small business here in Ottawa. I have two children and I'm legally separated. Why don't you give me a call [NUMBER] or at the office [NUMBER]."

FRANK assessment: Again, too short. Small business angle works, though.

• "Yes. Good afternoon. My name is [NAME]. It's Tuesday, February 1, 5:48 in the afternoon. I'm somewhat piqued by your ad and subsequent message. I seem to fit the bill, save and except for the Italian part, although I have a, uh, number of Italian clients. And I'm currently splitting my time between Toronto and Ottawa — uh, professional. And I, uh, can be reached on my Ottawa business line which is plugged into my cellular, preferably after 6:00 p.m. [NUMBER]."

FRANK assessment: Probably a lawyer. Anal-retentive attention to time/date and references to cell phone and Mafioso clientele bad signs. Avoid.

FRANK PRANKS

(March 17, 1994)
Zambonis up the Zambezi?

Given the performance of the Canadian International Development Agency (CIDA) in recent years, it's not much of a stretch to imagine them sending Zambonis to Evelyn Waugh country; in this case, the fictional East African Nation of Chapati. And given the Reform Party's stingy stance on foreign aid, we wondered how their MPs would respond to the news.

Masquerading as United Press Services, FRANK called up ten Reform Party MPs to get their response to the news story we invented. Each MP was told that CIDA had sent three ice-surfacing machines to Chapati.

Jack Ramsay (Crowfoot): Three ice-surfacing machines? Do they have ice surfaces over there?
FRANK: Not that I know of . . .
This is to where?
Chapati. It's a tropical climate . . .
Is it J-O-P-P?
No, C-H-A-P-A-T-I.
P-T-I. Oh, yes. Chapati. And that's in South Africa . . . that's in Africa?
East. East Africa.
And what department? What department sent them?
CIDA.

CIDA [LONG SIGH]. Well, this sounds like another irresponsible waste of taxpayers' money. We have heard that there's a number of Caterpillars sitting over there rusting in a, uh, foreign country, as well, and no one knows how—they've never ever been started up, and no one knows how to start them. And, apparently, this went through CIDA as well. So there's got to be a complete review of the mandate of CIDA to determine just what the taxpayer's money is being spent on. This is just absolutely outrageous. And this irresponsible attitude towards spending is why the country is in a half-a-trillion dollar debt hole and sinking. I would like to check further into this.

Herb Grubel (Capilano-Howe Sound): What is the average climate there?
FRANK: It's a tropical climate.
Yeah, I thought so.
It's not that far from Somalia.
I can't believe they would have hockey rinks. The energy consumption! Even in our latitude, it's very high for keeping an ice surface. To believe they would have three . . . I have been to Africa, and I'm completely stumped . . . is that part of the Sudan? I didn't know there was such a country. I spent a year in Nairobi, which is a capital

of a major country in Africa, and I don't think they had one ice rink. I would be very surprised. Maybe the Zambonis were modified to something else . . . The most recent issue of *Equinox* has — in fact I saw it on the airplane yesterday — a full story on what a Zamboni does.

Really?

You should have a look at it. It's *fascinating*. It talks about hockey and so on. It vacuums the damn place, it shaves it by a millimetre, it washes it, then it sprays ice on top of it, then it spreads it out with a blanket — all in one action. It's an amazing machine.

> It vacuums the damn place, it shaves it by a millimetre, it washes it, then it sprays ice on top of it, then it spreads it out with a blanket — all in one action. It's an amazing machine . . . Zzzzzzz.

Grubel: Pro-Zamboni

FRANK: As I'm sure you know, Chapati's human rights record is really atrocious.

Bob Mills (Red Deer, Reform foreign affairs critic): Sure, sure. I would question why [the Zambonis] are going there . . . We have to evaluate our trade-aid situation. More and more it's geared to "Can we get something out of it?" I'm not saying that's wrong, I just think we should call a spade a spade . . . Obviously, when it comes to human rights issues, that has to become a major concern.

What would be the party's position towards Chapati? Obviously, we feel it requires a total evaluation of the whole program. We would want to have each government evaluated . . . Let's look at it. If, in fact, there's major abuses there, I think that would weigh very heavily on not providing them with aid... Obviously, sending Zambonis anywhere would be totally out of the realm of what would seem reasonable.

Phil Mayfield (Cariboo-Chilcotin): **Where's Zampota?**
FRANK: It's Chapati.
Where is it?
Eastern Africa.
That's what I thought . . . Well, considering budgetary constraints we have as a country, and considering the machinery that's lined up in the jungle out there doing nothing because there are people who don't know how to operate it — I have not heard of ice machines being shipped from Canada to Africa before, but I'm astounded to hear it, I must say. Before you need an ice-surfacing machine, you have to have ice-making machines, don't you? Have we put in these arena and ice-making equipment?

FRANK: What do you think of CIDA funding going to Chapati?

Myron Thompson (Wild Rose): Well. [LONG PAUSE].
I should mention that they don't seem to have any ice over there, and these are ice-surfacing machines.
[LONG PAUSE] For the arenas? I don't know what to say. All I know is this government doesn't have much in the way of a priority list at all. I'm sure they need [the Zambonis] you know? [LAUGHS] But sometimes you just have to do without something. Are there other things the money could be spent on that could be of more value to the people who are in that, uh, reserve?

> Are there other things money could be spent on . . . in that, uh reserve?

Myron: The only good Zamboni...

FRANK PRANKS

Ted White (North Vancouver): It's not the sort of place you expect to find some ice. If you let your imagination run wild the obvious thing you think is, who over there has got the private ice rink and needs, uh, Zambonis?

Ken Epp (Elk Island): We should be concentrating on those areas whereby we can provide means so people in these under-developed countries can grow their own food. Probably recreation would be on a lower level of importance, I would think.

FRANK: Their human rights record isn't very good — political torture and executions, that kind of thing.

When that type of information becomes known, I think we should cut off all aid to those countries . . . If that's the case then I think that would be adequate reason not to give them anything, particularly not an ice-resurfacing machine. I would certainly want to investigate it further.

Dave Chatters (Athabasca): It sounds like a pretty off-the-wall idea in that part of the world. Ice resurfacing. It's one thing, the Caterpillars rusting away in parts of Africa under a CIDA program, but Zambonis in East Africa doesn't fit . . . I don't know how Zambonis will do a lot for empty bellies and starving people, but, you know, I'd have to look at what the program was supposed to be . . .

FRANK: Do you know anything about Chapati?

Grant Hill (Macleod): No, nothing.

I'm not a great internationalist, so I don't know anything about the country at all. [But] it's the same old story. If we are in debt to the tune of $500 billion, sending money anywhere — for anything — until we have our house in order, is almost nonsense to me.

Cliff Breitkreuz (Yellowhead): Ice-resurfacing machines in an African country? For what purpose?

FRANK: They're used to clean hockey rinks.

That's exactly it. I don't know of any African country that has a hockey team. So why would these machines be going over there? I think that whole organization [CIDA] has got to be reviewed.

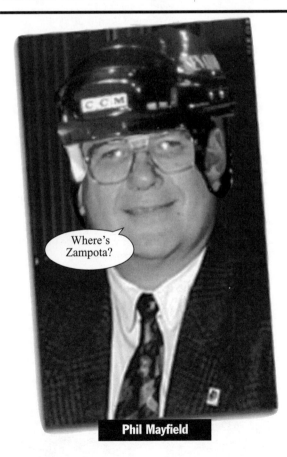

Phil Mayfield

Bob Mills

(May 12, 1994)
Fast Eddie Telephone Tag

Jean Crouton's chief of staff, Eddie Goldenberg, is among the heaviest hitters (biggest sticks, shurely?!— ed.) in the Liberal Party.

But how much pull does Eddie have in the Liberal cabinet? FRANK decided to test Eddie's clout with the ministers using the benchmark measure of Ottawa power politics — the speed with which one's telephone calls are returned.

FRANK masqueraded as Goldenberg's assistant and placed calls on his behalf to 17 Liberal cabinet ministers. We told their receptionists that we had "Eddie Goldenberg on the line for the minister."

(In the game of Hill telephone tag, the truly powerful never place their own calls.)

Then we started the stopwatch to see how long it would take to get through.

Of the 17 ministers we called, three dropped everything and got on the blower right away. FRANK/Eddie connected with Sheila Copps in a mere 27 seconds. We also immediately connected to Finance Minister Paul Martin and Indian Affairs Minister Ron Irwin. All three answered their private lines with a folksy, "Hello, Eddie."

Six other ministers called back within three hours, including Defence Minister David Collenette, who took time out from meeting with the Bosnian vice-president to return Eddie's call.

The only ministers who didn't return Eddie's call were three seasoned political vets: Treasury Board Minister Art Eggleton, Foreign Affairs Minister André Ouellet, and Public Works slaphead David Dingwall.

Those response times in full:

Lloyd Axworthy (Human Resources) — Assistant insisted on speaking directly to Goldenberg before putting the call through.
Doug Young (Transport) — Out of the country.
Ralph Goodale (Agriculture) — Out of country.
Sergio Marchi (Immigration) — Out of town.

Sheila Copps (Environment) — Connected in 27 seconds.
Paul Martin (Finance) — Connected in 35 seconds.
Ron Irwin (Indian Affairs) — Connected in 1 min, 10 seconds.
Michel Dupuy (Heritage) — Called back in 7 minutes.
Diane Marleau (Health) — Called back in 25 minutes.
David Collenette (Defence) — Called back in 36 minutes.
John Manley (Industry) — Called back in 2 hours.
Anne McLellan (Natural Resources) — Called back in 2 hours, 15 minutes.
Allan Rock (Justice) — Called back in 2 hours, 25 minutes (assistant asked correct spelling of Goldenberg)
Dave Dingwall (Public Works) — Did not return call.
Art Eggleton (Treasury) — Did not return call.
Andre Ouellet (Foreign Affairs) — Did not return call.
Brian Tobin (Fisheries) — Brother Terry Tobin called back in three minutes to ask how important the call was. When told it was extremely urgent, Tobin promised the minister would call from St. John's. He didn't.

The Winnah! (27 Seconds)

FRANK PRANKS

(June 9, 1994)
Reform Outing Shocker

When NDP MP Svend Robinson claimed "there are gay MPs in every federal party, except the Tories," ferocious speculation inside the Reform caucus began.

With the witch hunt underway, FRANK decided to stir up the pot by asking several Reformers if they were gay.

Posing as a reporter for the fictitious Moncton Tribune, *FRANK called several Reform MPs and told them that they had been "outed" by a Toronto gay rights organization. The Gay Empowerment Rights Bipartisan League (GERBiL) had issued a press release, they said, naming each of our victims as the gay members:*

FRANK: There's a gay rights organization in Toronto that's planning to out several MPs . . .

Elwin Hermanson (Kindersley-Lloydminster): Planning on what?
Outing. They say your name is on the list.
I guess I'm not overly concerned. I'm not in favour of taking away anyone's rights to equality . . . but there are safeguards for society that have to be put in place. I'm certainly not in favour of extra privileges for . . .
No, no, no . . .
. . . any group of people and I have a difficult time swallowing that gays and lesbians fall into a family category for biological reasons. So they may have put me on that list because I have these feelings.
No, I think maybe you're misunderstanding. When I say that they're "outing" MPs, they're saying that you're gay.

They're saying I'm gay? Oh. [LAUGHS] You better tell my wife that. That's absolutely wrong. No, I've never heard that term before, "outing." Oh, coming out of the closet? I see. No, it's not true. It never was and never will be.

FRANK: There's a gay rights association in Toronto and they say you're one of the gay members of the Reform caucus.
Bill Gilmour (Comox-Alberni): I'm certainly not gay. If I'm anything, I'm at the other end of the spectrum. I'm firmly in favour of the family. I've been married for 17 years, got a 14-year-old son. I've been a forester and a logger. It doesn't fit the right mould.
Do you know why they may have named you?
No. I find that most interesting. In fact, I'm thinking about my [constituency] office and I'm one of the few guys that has hired all women — two in this office and two in my Ottawa office.
Attractive women, are they?
Yeah, well, yeah. Both single in Ottawa. I have every eligible male zooming through my office. Twenty-four and twenty-nine-year-old single ladies.
Who else did they name?
Well, there's Svend Robinson, of course . . .
Svend for sure. And one of the Liberals — he sits in my row [in the House] down at the other end — made a statement, and his statement indicated to me that he kinda swings that way. It was on rights for same-sex marriages and this kind of thing.

Who was that?
I didn't look up the name. I know he's down at the end of the Bloc line, just at the edge of the Liberals, on our side of the floor. He didn't have an accent so I just assumed he was a Liberal.
Ed. note: The Liberals seated in Gilmour's row, next to the Bloc, were Paul Steckle (Huron-Bruce) and Brent St. Denis (Algoma).

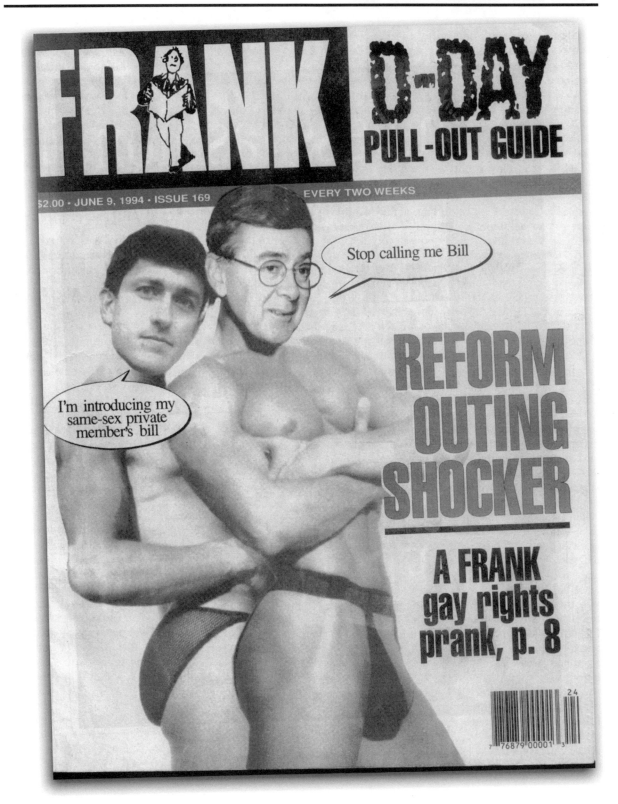

FRANK PRANKS

Jan Brown (Calgary-Southeast): That's the funniest thing I've ever heard in my life. My gosh. Well, I'm staggered.

FRANK: Any idea why they might have named you?

No. My male cousin died of AIDS in Vancouver just over a year ago. That's about the only thing I know of that they may have connected me to. I have gay friends, but I don't know — I'm very married for a long time . . . As I say, I do have some gay acquaintances in Ottawa, but doesn't everybody?

FRANK: It's a gay rights organization, the Gay Empowerment Rights Bipartisan League, and they've named you as one of the MPs in the Reform caucus who's gay.

Jim Silye (Calgary Centre): [HYSTERICAL LAUGHTER] I'd like you to fax it to me. [TELLS THE NEWS TO SOMEONE IN HIS OFFICE, MORE HYSTERICAL LAUGHTER] . . . The people who made that accusation are sick, perverted, and shouldn't deserve the space they occupy on whatever paper they're writing for. No, I'm a happily married man for 26 years, with two daughters. My oldest daughter just got married, and I would say these guys are guilty of not doing — well, they're guilty of lying, to begin with [MORE LAUGHTER]. Oh, shit, wait'll I get back to Ottawa. I can hear it now . . . You know, it's interesting, I gave a Let's Talk newsletter out here in Calgary Centre. I came out in favour of including sexual orientation in the Charter, because I don't feel you should dis-criminate on, you know, any grounds. But I also go on to say that's based on individual rights, and our laws in our society are based on heterosexual society.

Homosexuals, therefore, do not qualify for those same rights. Therefore, I'm against same-sex spousal benefits, same-sex marriages and adoption by homosexuals. So I've said that publicly here in Calgary, so I have no idea where they would get this. [LAUGHS] Of all the people to be accused of . . .

FRANK: Apparently, they issued a press release naming the gay MPs on the Hill and they've got you on the list.

Randy White (Fraser Valley West): [LAUGHS] Don't be ridiculous. You're talking about gay or anti-gay? Well, gay. Any reason you could think of why they may have named you?

Because I'm one of the more anti-gay people. I'd like to know where they get the nerve to do that . . . I have two female members in the office who'd just love to hear that news. No thanks, I think I'll bypass that offer. No, if anything, I'm just the opposite of that. I'm not for gay rights at all. Anyone in this town knows my position . . . Boy did they pick the wrong guy.

Garry Breitkreuz (Yorkton-Melville): You're not serious! The gay rights people put out a press release — it was Svend Robinson?

No, this organization, independent of Robinson, named you.

I'm absolutely flabbergasted. I have no idea where — I'm speechless.

Is there any truth to it?

No, absolutely not. You want to talk to my wife?

No, it's okay.

I find this absolutely ludicrous. I'm just floored. I heard before that they suspected some Reform MPs were gay and I thought "Yeah, right." I know them all. If they thought I was one, they have absolutely no idea . . . Of course, they're trying to promote their narrow agenda and they're trying to get as much sympathy as they can.

Note: The fun ends when Kevin Gaudet, a brownshirt in Jan Brown's office, smells a rat and called to find out what was going on. We brush him off with some dextrous faux call-waiting work. But minutes later, calls go out to Reform members warning them to refuse questions from the Moncton Tribune. *Gaudet later calls back demanding to know where the* Tribune *is located. When we tell him it's in Chapati, he catches on and asks when the next issue of FRANK comes out.*

Jan, Garry: They're here . . .

(September 1, 1994)
This Hour Has Seven Duhs

This summer's mania for silver anniversaries — Woodstock, the moon landings, Charles Manson popping his head pipes — had us fondly recalling a particularly Canadian icon from the sixties, This Hour Has Seven Days. *The weekly current affairs show, hosted by Patrick Watson, Laurier LaPierre and Dinah Christie (pre-Scientology wig-out) had a critically acclaimed two-year run on CBC before it was pulled off the air amidst bitter acrimony and finger-pointing.*

For the thirtieth anniversary of the Seven Days *debut (Oct. 4), wouldn't it be fun if the program was resurrected from its grainy, black and white grave with a new set of hosts? With that premise in mind, we set up a bogus production company, wrote ourselves a deal with a "major network" and began trolling for bingo-callers. Here's a few excerpts from our telephone talent search.*

Elwy Yost. Host of TVOntario's *Saturday Night at the Movies.* **(We reach Elwy after first talking to his wife.)**
FRANK: Mr. Yost. I'm calling from Minotaur Productions in Ottawa.
Yost: Oh, could you wait until I get some clothes on? I thought you would be tied up so I went into the bathroom. Just one second. [PAUSE OF AP- PROXIMATELY ONE MINUTE]...
Hello? [To wife] Lila you can hang up, dear. Yes, my friend, what can I do for you?
FRANK: Well, we've obtained the rights to *This Hour Has Seven Days*, the old CBC current affairs show.
Oh my God!
FRANK: We're putting together a pilot this spring and are looking for possible hosts. Your name came up as someone who might be available.
My God. Well, I'm very honoured. It's one of my favourite shows. They're bringing it back, eh? . . . I am freelance, [but] I should check with TVOntario. To avoid personal nightmares, I should check with them, to be fair.
FRANK: This would be quite different from what you're doing now . . . Is this something you'd be interested in?
Well, of course I am. I'm just wondering though, God, if you'd be better to get a Patrick Watson or

This Hour Has Seven Duhs

somebody sort of more tuned to the world.

FRANK: Well, Mr. Shapiro, our executive producer specifically asked that we call you.

My goodness. Isn't that wonderful. What's his first name?

FRANK: Robert.

Robert Shapiro. I've heard that name. Oh, gosh, yes. Well I'd certainly be interested, yes . . . I think it's so exciting. *This Hour Has Seven Days* has always been one of my favourite shows.

FRANK: What kind of experience do you have in current affairs?

No, nothing. See, that's the thing. I've never had any experience in current affairs. I'm a university graduate in sociology and I read, so I'm reasonably well up on things. I love interviewing and so forth, but I'm not a current affairs specialist. Do you have any idea what you're paying? What sort of range? Any thought about that?

FRANK: I'm not really at liberty to discuss — I'd imagine we'd be paying at the higher end of what you'd expect, because it is a network show.

. . . It might even behoove me to leave TVOntario if I ever got [the job] . . . I'm certainly interested. Yeah, let's leave it at that for the moment. And honoured. And please give my best to Mr. Shapiro.

FRANK: He says he's met you a few times, actually.

What's his first name?

FRANK: Robert.

Robert. Yes, we must have. I don't know a lot, but we must have. The name stands out. I guess professionally I know him, too. My very best to him. I'm honoured I'd even be considered, my goodness.

Jim Tatti. Co-host of Global Television's *Sportsline.*

FRANK: Are you familiar with the old CBC program, *This Hour Has Seven Days*?

Not really.

FRANK: It was a current affairs show

that ran in the sixties, quite successful. Our company has the rights to the name and we're doing a remake. Is this the sort of thing you'd be interested in?

Yeah. It's the same idea, though — current affairs?

FRANK: Yeah.

Yeah, sure. I'm more than interested in that.

FRANK: What are your contractual obligations with Global?

I don't really have any. I'm sort of a staff member. I'm wide open to just about anything. They do allow me to do freelance for other stations depending on the specific project.

FRANK: This is a fairly large production. I don't imagine you'd have a lot of time to do anything on the side.

Then I'm interested. I'm always looking for changes to my lifestyle. I've been working until midnight every night for eleven years — cramped out a bit. I'm open for that.

Tom Gibney. Co-host of CFTO evening news and the host of the Lotto 6/49 telecasts.

Gibney: I haven't had that much [interviewing experience] in the past while, I must be honest with you. But in the years gone by I have. I have done an interview show — with a very small audience. Other than that, I've done just about everthing else.

FRANK: Were you involved in a lotto?

Oh, yes. Lotto 6/49. I've done that for eleven years. You're not familiar with Lotto 6/49?

FRANK: Uh, is that the Fay

Dance thing?

Not that one.

That one is Win-TV. I was doing that one up until last month and then I quit. It wasn't worth it. No, this one is Wednesday and Saturday nights. We stand there in front of this silly machine that's going around and around dropping numbers and people are getting rich except me. What I do is I front the show — it's only a five minute show. I call out the numbers, the prize money and so on, and that's it.

FRANK: It's a bingo-calling kinda thing?

Well, the numbers are pre-picked. In essence, the draw is made and I marry what I do live with watching the video of the draw. I've been doing that for eleven years. It used to be seen across Canada up until about three years ago, then they decided to cut back on the costs. The only people that carry it now is CFCF-Montreal. Thank God for the French.

Allan Fotheringham. *Maclean's* columnist and *Front Page Challenge* panelist. Fotheringham: I used to co-host CKVU Darrel Duke's — it was the first independent station in Vancouver with Laurier LaPierre. I've done TV for years.

FRANK: We're putting together a pilot in the spring of next year. What's your availability like?

I'm not sure I'm going to be alive in the spring of next year . . . I do, at the moment, *Front Page Challenge* . . . We tape every second week in Vancouver.

That's my only commitment. October to December.

FRANK: I think you'd find that what we have planned would be very time consuming. It wouldn't allow you the opportunity for other projects on the side. That's a long way away. We think they're going to kill off the show every year and we're surprised by the fact that they continued it this year. I think it's on its last legs.

FRANK: How would you feel about a co-host?

That would be okay, if it was somebody of equal stature and [who] I could get on with.

FRANK: Any names come to mind?

Well, Pam Wallin. Someone of that stature. There's a very good guy in Vancouver, works for CBC. Ian Hanomansing, his name is. He's from India or Sri Lanka, or something like that *(Halifax, actually — ed.)*. Very handsome guy. He's somebody you could look at. He's a real bright up-and-comer.

FRANK: What's your interest in doing a show like this?

Anything that could be anywhere the equal of *This Hour Has Seven Days* — anybody in the country would leap at the idea if you could duplicate or replicate the sort of thing they did. Sure, I'd be interested. I prefer the one-on-one stuff rather than what I do now on *Front Page* which is four people, so you only get a minute or two with each guest, which is frustrating. I prefer to have a good chew at it for 15 minutes . . . There's no law that says I have to stay with [*Front Page*].

Jeanne Beker. CityTV reporter and host of syndicated *Fashion Television*.

FRANK: Is this something you'd feel comfortable with?

Beker: Well, yeah. I don't know. I'd have to find out more about it and more about the people who are putting it together and the format it would take. You say hard-core and investigative reporting?

FRANK: Well, you'd be doing mostly interviews. You'd have lots of producers working on your behalf. That's something I'm very comfortable with. You're talking about the possibility of launching into somewhat of a new direction, even though I certainly have a profile. I certainly have a high visibility. I certainly have not made my name interviewing politicians. But on the other hand, I'm a professional and a journalist. I've been on camera for 15 years in this country and State-side.**

Ralph Benmurgui. Former host of *Friday Night! with Ralph Benmergui.*

FRANK: We're trying to emulate the original program.

You're going to call it *This Hour Has Seven Days*? Wow, that's fabulous [LAUGHS]. It's like painting a target on yourself at this point, but it should be fun. Yeah, sure. If [Shapiro] wants to give me a call and talk about, I'd be interested in talking about it.

FRANK: What are you doing right now?

I'm just doing some radio and writing a book. And other than that I'm just talking to a few people about some different ideas but that's about it. I've talked to *Newsworld* about something, but nothing more than just talk. That's about it.

FRANK: What's the book about?

Me. Little old me. It's called *Who Do You Think You Are?*

Peter Feniak. Former co-host of *Lifetime*.

FRANK: Is this the kind of thing for him?

Angela Wright (Feniak's agent): Oh, definitely. He's a journalist. His background is journalism. He's been writing pieces for the *Toronto Star* .. . He's done a lot of shows where he's interviewed all kinds of people. Some celebrities but also politicians and things like that. He's very smart, a very warm individual. I've got some of his famous [interviews] on tape. I must admit I can't remember who they are at this second — Mila Mulroney.

FRANK: Would he be willing to cut his hair? He has very long hair.

No, no, no. He never had long hair. He may have had it slightly below his collar. But now it's a regular IBM haircut. He's a very corporate-looking person.

Stu Jeffries. Former host of *Good Rockin' Tonight* and *Switchback*.

FRANK: What kind of current affairs does Stu have?

Monica Hubert (Jeffries's agent): Well, with his radio show he [has] talked for three months. He's looking for more challenging things . . . Is this one that Vicki Gabereau was involved with?

FRANK: No, it was Laurier LaPierre and Patrick Watson. It was a current affairs show.

I think actually [Stu] would be wonderful. I think what I might do is send you a tape of his radio show. Radio's live, you know. During *Good Rockin'* he interviewed everybody who was anybody but it was all cut together and it wasn't live. It was kind of hard to see his interviewing skills. When he had the talk show on the radio he was fabulous.

FRANK PRANKS

(April 26, 1995)

Save the Sushi

With Brian Tobin waging war on the Spanish in the Maritimes, FRANK decided to open a Western Front and take on the Japanese fishing industry.

Hoping to provoke an Estai-like incident, we invented the Pacific Fisheries Coalition, and then called up several landlubber Reform MPs to ask what they thought about Japanese overfishing of our sushi stocks.

We didn't tell them, of course, that sushi is not a fish at all but a type of food consisting of a variety of fish served raw on rice.

The following are excerpts from our Reform fish files:

FRANK: I'm with a group that represents about 4,000 fishermen. And we're hoping to raise awareness of the problem of Japanese overfishing of sushi stocks.

Ken Epp (Elk Island): Oh, so we have it going on the West coast, too. It's worse than the problem out East with cod or turbot. Our scientific reports indicate that the sushi stocks will be extinct within about five years if the Japanese don't stop overfishing. **I wasn't even aware. I heard that there had been some problems with respect to the United States encroaching into our territory. I don't know any of the details. Fishing isn't my specialty . . .**

SAVE THE SUSHI

I'm really going to show my ignorance here — is the name of the fish actually "sushi?"
Well, there is a fish. The sushi fish. There are also several fish that are related — mackerel, for instance, is a common sushi dish. It's a $500-million industry. There's a real increased popularity of sushi restaurants in Canada. We're worried that, in a few years from now, if the Japanese continue to overfish, we're not going to be able to meet our demand.
I guess we need to talk about it. I cannot at this

Epp

stage express an opinion on how it should be handled. Undoubtedly, we need to pay some pretty close attention to preserving our resources for the future. In that regard, we have a fair degree of support for what Tobin is doing out on the East Coast. If the nations in total don't take any action, who's going to be fishing? Nobody is going to be fishing. We need to look at that, in the long run.

FRANK: The Japanese are creating a real problem and our information is that the sushi stocks could

be extinct in five years.
Ed Harper (Simcoe Centre): Oh, is that right? I must admit that it is an issue I must look into, then. This is the first time I've been made aware that it's close to becoming extinct. I didn't appreciate the magnitude of the overfishing.
It's funny. A lot of people don't even think of sushi because it is a dish that is sort of exotic.
Yeah, yeah. That's right. When you talked about a half-a-billion, I had no idea.
Do you eat sushi?
No, just occasionally. It's an hors d'ouevre but it's not something that's a regular diet, no.
Increasingly, in Canada, people are eating more. The demand is going up.
The danger is close, you think?

Momson

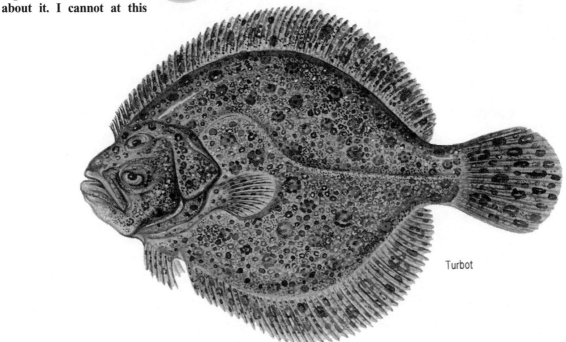

Turbot

FRANK PRANKS

(July 5, 1995)
Registration = Castration

Say "No" to Gun Control

Our American cousins have seen the National Rifle Association flex its celebrity might with endorsements from the likes of Charlton Heston and Ronnie Reagan.

To find out who, if anyone, would publicly align themselves against Allan Rock's gun control legisla-tion, FRANK invented an organiza-tion called the Canadian Coalition of Responsible Gun Owners, then began trolling for a home-grown celeb to appear in our advertising campaign. First on our list was an easy mark . . .

FRANK: I'm with the Canadian Coalition of Responsible Gun Owners. We're a lobby group based in Ottawa. We're looking for someone to appear in our television and radio commercials. Your name came up as someone who might be interested.
Ernst Zundel (Holocaust denier): I have to tell you, I wouldn't know which way of the gun is up. I don't own a gun, I have never owned a gun. And you realize that if the me-dia — they will say, "Oh, they have that Carlton Street fascist."
Well, that's okay. We want an icon-oclastic spokesman. Our slogan is, "Registration Equals Castration." What kind of appearance fee would you require?
I wouldn't want any, if it is a cause I believe in.
You understand we are opposed to the gun registry?
Yes, and I agree with you. You think that criminals on the street with Saturday Night Specials are going to register their guns? No, I agree with you.

FRANK: I'm with the Coalition of Responsible Gun Owners and . . .
Mr. McCartney (agent for Al Waxman): The Polish?
No. The Coalition of Responsible Gun Owners. We're a lobby group. We're kicking off our media campaign and our executive has mentioned Al Waxman as a person who might be appropriate for us. I was wondering about his availability.
So far, it's hard to say. He's in the movie business and he just finished three movies in the last six weeks. He's off to Europe for two weeks to do a movie and after that, I don't know. He used to, I think at one point. He has done a lot of stuff like that in the past.
Any military service?
I don't know. Isn't that bizarre?
What kind of ballpark would we be looking at for two or three days work?
It's not the two or three days work. It's the amount of profile he would be giving the group.
I understand.
It's his expertise and profile.

FRANK: Jeff Healey's name came up and we were wondering if he'd be available for this kind of thing?
Dawna Zeema (agent for Healey): You are with a group of responsible gun owners? I'd have to find out how he felt about that. What exactly is your campaign?
We're lobbying against gun registration.
What's involved with him?
We'd like him to appear in our televi-sion and radio ads. Whatever format he feels comfortable with. Something that would play on his reputation and his personality.
I can talk to him to see if he is interested.
Does he hunt at all?
No, he doesn't.
Are any of his band members hunters?
Uh, no, not that I'm aware of.
Does he own a gun?
Uh, no. Canadians don't, though I could be wrong [UNINTELLI-GIBLE].
Just so that we're not wasting each others' time, what sort of ballpark, in terms of endorsement fees?
I'd have to ask him that.

Bruce Davidson (agent to beloved kiddie star Eric Nagler): Why would you use Eric?
He has a good presence. He's very popular among the people on our executive who suggested him.
[LONG PAUSE] We're open for anything. Yes. We'd be open for a presentation on that, as long as he doesn't have to get up and start handling guns. You're talking about children and guns. The farther away you keep children and guns, the better, as far as we're concerned.
Sure. We feel that could be part of our campaign, as well. Our slogan is, "Guns don't kill people, murderers kill people." Who else does he endorse?

HE'S NOT FUNNY.
NEITHER IS GUN REGISTRY.

The Liberal government has passed legislation that will force law-abiding Canadians to register their guns. Next they'll force us to watch *Air Farce*. Tell Allan Rock he can have your gun only when he can pry it out of your cold, dead fingers. Protest the Liberal gun registry.

Dave Broadfoot's appearance in this advertisement is in no way representative of the opinions of either the Royal Canadian Mounted Police or the Canadian Broadcasting Company.

PAID FOR BY THE CANADIAN COALITION OF RESPONSIBLE GUN OWNERS

FRANK PRANKS

He's worked with Proctor and Gamble. He's worked with Pampers. We've been approached by a large bank to do some business with them. Eric has to feel comfortable about it. If it was something that was loaded with sugar and guaranteed to create zits, we're not really excited about that. But Kellogg's Corn Flakes, we have no problem with.

We're looking at about $25,000 for the appearance. Is that sort of in his ball park?

Yup. Yup. It depends on positioning and how you do it. As soon as you say "guns and children" all the little red flags go up in the back of my head. It's really important to remember that Eric has a huge constituency with families across this nation, both for and against [gun control]. You would have to make sure he totally understands both sides of the issue and be able to defend that he is doing these commercials. It has got to feel right to everybody.

One of the reasons his name came up is that we felt that he has a family values appeal, but we wouldn't want to mix children into the ads.

Be aware that you can't help it. He's Eric from *Eric's World*. You can't help that.

Maybe we can work that in, in a tasteful way. Does he do any hunting?

No, I don't think he does. Some people don't play golf. I don't hunt. I play golf. A lot of musicians are like that. They're not for or against it, it just isn't part of their lifestyle.

FRANK: What is [Dave Broadfoot's] availability right now?

Donna Trimble (agent for Broadfoot): He's doing live shows right now, sort of traveling the country. And dinner guest appearances, that sort of thing.

Does he do other endorsements?

He hasn't done anything for quite some time.

Do you know if he hunts?

I don't know.

One thing we were thinking of is the Mountie character. Is that a proprietary thing? Could he do that for one of the spots?

I'm not sure. I don't know if he owns that character. That's something he did with the *Air Farce*. You might be getting into all sorts of copyright infringement. I'm not sure he would agree to do this as a character, but he might do it as Dave Broadfoot. You see what I'm

saying?

Yeah. The Mountie would be great, though, if we could. It's such an icon.

The Mountie. I don't know if we can. Dave Broadfoot as Dave Broadfoot is one thing. But when he has to go into character, that would be different.

Let's step back for a minute. Is there anyone else you represent who might be more appropriate.

[LONG PAUSE] No. Not with this issue. It's a very touchy issue.

What sort of ballpark are you in, in terms of fees?

Well, there are ACTRA minimums, but Dave is well above that. It would be some sort of negotiated fee. It really depends. What's in your budget. What were you thinking?

We were thinking 25 to 30 for the three days.

Twenty-five to 30.

Thousand.

For the three days.

Yes.

And so what appeals to you is his Mountie character? You want him to do it as the Mountie. That's your preference?

That's our preference – unless he had another character, who would be more sympathetic, like a hunter character. Is that the right range, though?

Oh, God. Yeah. You're in a nice range for him.

(August 30, 1995)

Psychic Predictions

Will Paul Bernardo beat the murder rap? When will Fat Jack Parizeau call the referendum? Will Robbie Alomar really abandon the sadsack Blue Jays?

To answer these burning questions, FRANK called several psychic hotlines and, equipped with the appropriate astrological data, posed as various Great Canadians™ with questions on their minds. Here's what transpired:

JOHN ROSER
(Lawyer for Baul Bernardo)
DENMARK DIAL LIVE PSYCHIC LINE: What's your first name?
FRANK: John. I'm having some professional problems. I'm a lawyer and I have this difficult client I'm representing in a murder trial. I'm feeling a little bit guilty about representing him because I'm pretty sure he's guilty.
So, what's your question?
I'm trying to decide two things — whether I should put him on the stand or not, and also, I want to know if he's going to get off.
What's his name?
Paul.
Ask me another question while I shuffle the cards.
I'm concerned that if I represent him to the best of my ability, he's going to get off.
But you have to do your job.
I have to do my job. Yeah. [Long pause at $3.99 a minute] You're doing tarot cards?
Yeah. Okay, the first card is

[UNINTELLIGIBLE] of Wands, and that came up reversed. So, this could be problems involving your pride. This will test your inner strength. Your other concern is the reversed Ace of Pentacles. So you could be approaching it from the wrong direction. Are you thinking of putting him on the stand?
Yeah, I'm thinking about it. You don't think I should?
Well, from the card, it looks like maybe not. The immediate past is the Three of Pentacles, and that's

the skilful use of your abilities. The immediate future is the Magician card, and that's reversed, so all your abilities and strengths — you may be kind of misusing them. What you have to work with right now is the Four of Wands and that's reversed, so you may be showing a bit of a threat to your security. You don't want to look unsuccessful, for your own reputation.
Do you think he's going to get off?
I'm not really sure. Is there a woman involved?
Yeah, Karla.
Involved with you or with him?
With him. Or she was. Not any more.
Do you think she knows something she's not saying?
She has testified in the trial.
It looks like her testimony will decide it. The card that represents your relationship to the question is the Page of Wands, and that's reversed, so that could be some bad news — insincerity, maybe on your own part.
So if you had to go by what you see now, which way do you think it would go?
Probably that he would not get off.
Because of her?
Yeah.

JACQUES PARIZEAU
LATOYA JACKSON'S PSYCHIC NETWORK: Can I have the date of your birth, Jacques?
FRANK: August 9, 1930.
And what are you calling in concern of?
Well, I'm involved in politics and I'm trying to decide on a date for a rather important vote. I have committed to a date

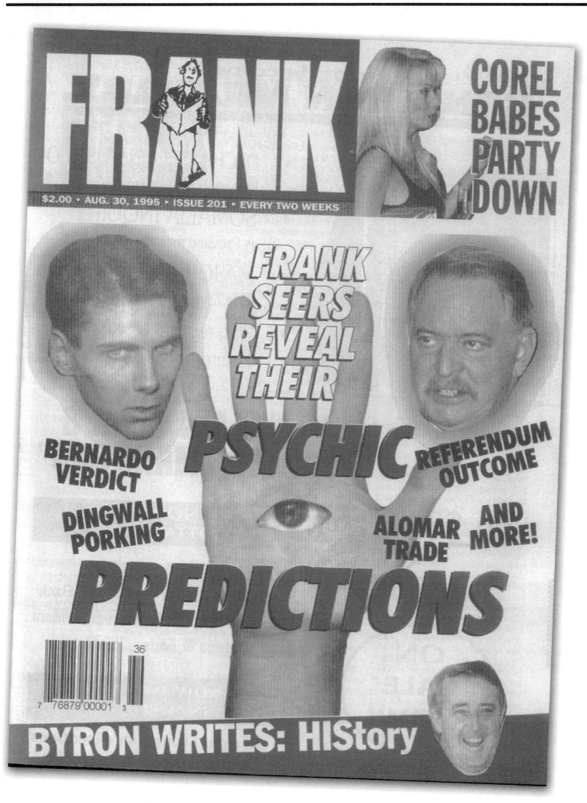

in the fall, but I haven't decided on which exact date.

Okay, let me ask, what exactly is this, or is it confidential?

It's a provincial referendum on the future of the province. I have to choose a date to go to the polls.

Let me tune in and see what would be the best time for you [LONG PAUSE] I feel that you should move after the year.

After the year?

Yes, when the new year is in.

Oh, really. Why?

I give you the time to move should be in the first week of 1996.

So, the first couple of days in January? There is a certain result I want. I want a "Yes" vote. Any day in particular that's most likely to give me that?

A lot of people are not going to go for the move.

Really? What percentage will, the way it is now? Less than half?

Ten out of 20 will go for it. And it is showing that 15 out of 20 would go for it in January.

What if I had it in the fall?

They wouldn't really go for it. They would want to keep it a little longer.

ROBERTO ALOMAR

FRANK: My name is Robbie. I'm an athlete and I'm thinking of leaving the team I'm playing for. I'm trying to decide whether I should do it.

LATOYA JACK-SON'S PSYCHIC NETWORK: Who do you play for?

A baseball team in Toronto.

What makes you feel you want to change it?

Well, the team is playing really badly and I'd rather play for a winning team,

because I'm having a good season. This team I play for is in last place.

Do other people want to hire you?

Yeah, there are other teams I could play for.

Well, my advice to you is to go along with another team because I'm showing that that is going to become successful for you.

Any idea where I should try to play? Any cities that you think would be good for me?

Well, sweetie, what I'm feeling you should do is pay very close mind, very close attention, because some people, yes, will be out there to make you part of the team, make you feel comfortable. And some just want to use you as a product. You have to use your own judgment.

You think Boston, maybe?

Maybe.

DAVID DINGWALL

INVISION PSYCHICS: Hi, this is Ron. I'll be doing your reading. Can I have your first name and date of birth?

FRANK: Dave. June 29, 1952 . . . I work in government and I'm concerned that I'm going to lose my job in the near future. There have been suggestions of misconduct, that I directed government money to some friends. I'm worried.

What's your hair and eye colour?

My hair is, uh, dark. My eyes are brown.

Let me concentrate on this [LONG PAUSE] I won't say anything about your degree of guilt right now. Does this involve other people you are working with?

Well, yes. I redirected some project money to some people I know, back

in my home province of Nova Scotia.

Was this flat-out bad, or, how do I put this? I get the feeling this wasn't flat-out wrong on your part.

No, it wasn't. But that's the perception, and that's why I'm worried I'll lose my job.

Is there an inquiry process going on already?

There may be an internal inquiry. It's not public.

It's sort of vague right now. The way things look, the whole inquiry process is going to take a while. I'm getting the feeling that, overall, it's going to be tight, it's going to be ugly, but you're going to get off the hook. Was this going on for a fair while?

Uh, yeah.

You really got lucky in the past couple of times. There were at least two or three times you could have been caught.

Do you think I will lose my job?

This is leading up to the inquiry process itself. Do you know who will be heading it? There could be a man involved, in the process, and I don't know if he is specifically out to get you, or if he is out to get people who are accused of this sort of thing. There's going to be a guy like that who will be real trouble for you.

Mitchell Sharp, maybe.

Yeah, it looks like it's going to be miserable. Thus far, it looks like you are going to be off the hook. But it's far from certain.

PETER MANSBRIDGE

EVANLY-RAY'S PSYCHIC LINE: [Tedious exchange of astrological info excised] What's your question, Peter?

I'm living with a woman right now, and I'm trying to decide whether or not we should get married. Her name is Cynthia.

Yes, you are thinking about it.

FRANK PRANKS

That's for sure. You are possibly into advertising, journalism, something like that?
I'm in journalism.
Hmmm. Go out to a party, for crying out loud. It's a party time of year. You have Mars and Libra. You have it, natally, and you also have it by transit. Now the big problem with Mars — the giddy-up and go energy — it can be aggression and strife, and it's in the sign of relationships, which is Libra.
Okay.
What a person has to do is learn to do is make sure you are aggressively cooperative, not competitive.
What does this mean with respect to Cynthia?
Right at this time, I would say don't fall completely into a partnership. Don't give away all of your energy. You like women who display a spirit of fun and independence, but you are also attracted to women who like to roam, who are out there in society.
Well, she's an actress.
Oh, well, there you go. That's a Leo thing. Right now there is this love thing. Venus is coming through Leo.
Right.
The big thing is, in relationships, you were born in the generation with Neptune in Libra. Now, Neptune means idealism. Sometimes with that position, we are trying to escape into a relationship, or out of a relationship.
I was divorced a few years ago.
Right. You've got to stop and look and see about your individuality in this relationship. Are you giving away a whole lot

of energy?
Uh, I don't think so.
Well, otherwise, it looks very good. If you use temperance and a little bit of judgment, I can see peaceful skies coming.

KIM CAMPBELL
ZENOBIA
PSYCHIC LINE:
Hello, this is Sybiline. What is your name.
FRANK: Kim Campbell . . . I'm at a career crossroads. I worked in politics for a long time, and now I'm temporarily working as a broadcaster. I'm looking for some direction about which lines of work I should pursue.
Okay. Now the first thing I'm noticing — I haven't even got [the tarot cards] all laid out yet — the first thing to remember is to keep your attitude really positive. There are opportunities and there is a man

associated with you in some way who can be very beneficial to you.
Yes, Gregory.
Keep your attitude up. When you start getting it pulled down, bad things happen . . . [several minutes of positive attitude nonsense excised here].
These cards look good. They show here that you will have two opportunities, two different choices to make. You have a King of Cups, and he is a really nice man. You will have a decision to make with him. And then, within two weeks, another person will contact you about something to make money or do a new project.
Okay.
Then it says you will have — this may already have happened — you had a personal disappointment that really upset you. It didn't work out the way you planned it to. But it says to keep a good attitude about the situation. In two weeks, there is another offer of money and another situation.
Is there any indication I should lean towards broadcasting?
There is a lot of opportunity. I have a feeling you will drop into it. Both politics and broadcasting look good. Broadcasting because you love it. And politics, because there is going to be an opportunity there. It shows a man. He is a different one than the other man.
Does he have curly hair?
I don't know.

(December 17, 1995)

FRANK plays bagman for Muldoon's Airbus defence fund

"I Gave at the Office"

As the clouds of Airbus darkness gather over Byron Muldoon, his former colleagues and political cronies are left with difficult choices. Do they a) step forward to pledge public support of the ex-PM, b) distance themselves as quickly as possible, or c) cower in the shadows and hope nobody asks their opinion?

When he was prime minister, Muldoon never tired of reminding his caucus colleagues about the value of loyalty and fidelity and how "Ya dance with the one who brung ya!" ("No whore like an old whore!" shurely!? –ed.).

To gauge the level of support among Muldoon amigos, we called up a gaggle of former cabinet ministers, senators, and hangers-on, then asked them to put their money where their mouths were.

Posing as a bagman for "The Nova Fund," FRANK begged these top Tories for donations to help pay Mulroney's legal bills.

FRANK: I'm with the Nova Fund. I'm calling on a matter of some confidentiality. We've set up a collective of friends and colleagues of Mr. Mulroney. We're trying to raise some money to help underwrite the cost of his legal defence. I was wondering if you were in a position to help him out?

Barbara McDougall (Appointed Minister of Employment by Muldoon in 1988): [LONG SIGH IN BEST *DOUBLE EXPOSURE* IMITATION] Well, it would be small. I mean, I'm not – you know – I'm quite happy to help. I would certainly want my name on it.

Sure.

I'm not a corporate giant.

Sure. I understand.

Listen, could you call me at my office next Monday? I'm hardly in this week.

You know what I could do? I could just put you down for a really small amount.

Okay, and then just send me what-ever I need to know.

I can put you down for $25.

Oh, it will be more than that, but not much.

Okay.

Um, put me down for $50 and I'll see when I go through if I can do a little bit more.

Okay, that's terrific. Thank-you.

BABS MCDOUGALL "PUT ME DOWN FOR $50"

FRANK: Might you be able to help us out?

Michael Cogger (appointed to the senate by Muldoon in 1986) Heh, heh. I'm afraid I can't. No offence, and please – if I could, if I can, I will. Right now, my own circumstances – as you may know, or you may not know – I have had to pay – to look at – very hefty legal bills myself.

Sure. Yes, I understand.

My case was heard in appeal about three weeks ago. So, that sort of dug into my own meagre resources. But, let me, nevertheless, because one can always hope that things will change – where would I get you?

You could contact Roger Tassé, [ADDRESS].

Brian is well aware of my own circumstances.

Even a small, token donation?

It's a bit ironic because, God knows, I would like to. He helped me look after my own lawyers.

Even a small amount. We could put you down for $25.

Let me see and I will do my utmost.

FRANK: I was wondering if you might be able to help us out.

Joe Clark (former Prime Minister): [LONG PAUSE] You better send me a note, if you don't mind.

Okay, sure.

My fax number is (403) 290-4265.

Do you think you might be able to give us a hand?

Well, let me take a look at what you – at your note.

FRANK: Did your secretary explain why I'm calling?

Bill Thorsell (editor of *The Globe*): Yes. Uh, I'm not really in a position, given my news role, to be able to participate in that, although I think the cause is a very good one.

Right.

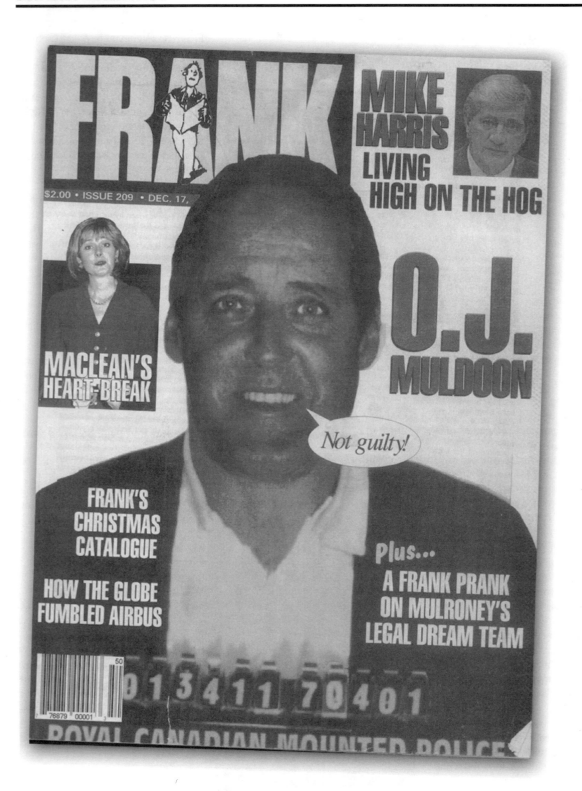

Uh, I just have to stay away from the substance of the things we cover.

I understand that. I wasn't asking for a donation from the *Globe and Mail*, per se. Even a personal donation . . .

Yeah, but even there – if that were found to be true, it would cause a big problem, I think, for us.

I can't stress enough how confidential this whole matter is. We're not giving tax receipts. Even a small donation . . .

It just puts me in a conflict-of-interest, though. And I just can't be in those situations. So, sometimes [LAUGHS] it's a good excuse. Actually, it's not an excuse, it's a real issue.

Sure, sure.

This is a very big story and we have to keep covering it. God knows where it will go, and what will all happen. I just can't be a partisan in any way, myself, in the story.

Could I rely on you not to mention this to anyone?

Yeah.

I guess being at a newspaper, you are conflicted in this . . .

No, I won't mention this to a soul. I think it's a perfectly honourable and good thing you are doing. The fact that you talked to me about it doesn't expose you to anything.

Great.

Sorry I can't help you.

FRANK: As you are probably aware, Mr. Mulroney is incurring heavy legal costs right now.

Bill McKnight (Appointed Minister of Defence by Mulroney in 1989): I wouldn't be surprised.

The feeling among people we've talked to is that we don't want to see the former prime minister bled dry

BILL McKNIGHT "I JUST DON'T KNOW"

by this. We're talking to friends and colleagues to see if they might be able to help us out with a donation.

Uh, I'll try to do it. I just invested a whole ton into a business in Saskatchewan. Give me your address.

It's the Nova Fund, [GIVES ADDRESS]. How much do you think you'll be able to contribute?

I just don't know. Everything is into this business, and it's just in start up, so I'll be very cautious. But I'll see what can be done.

Any amount. Mr. Mulroney understands that different people have different business obligations.

All right.

SEN. Gerry St. Germain (Appointed to the Senate by Muldoon in 1993): Well, I'm definitely prepared to help out but, do I know you?

FRANK: Uh, no. We've never met.

I'm always prepared to help a friend out. I'd like to know a little more about what's going on. But as far as the principle of the thing – helping somebody – I'm definitely prepared to help somebody, him especially.

We're trying to raise $500,000 and we've got about 200 names on

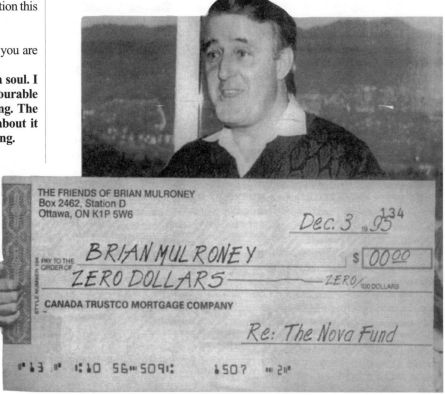

FRANK PRANKS

JOE CLARK
"SEND ME A NOTE"

MICHEL COGGER
"I WILL DO MY UTMOST"

BILL THORSELL
"IT'S A PERFECTLY HONOURABLE AND GOOD THING YOU ARE DOING"

our list so anything you could help us out with we'd appreciate. Do you know how much you could contribute?

How much? I want to talk to a few people first. I want to look at the whole thing before I make any commitment on the phone. I don't doubt you, but you could be the press.

FRANK: Could you make a donation to help the former prime minister.

Paul Dick (appointed Minister of Supply and Service by Muldoon in 1989): I'm still trying to get a full-time job, so I don't have the money to do that right now. I'm sorry. No way.

Any amount would help…

[ANGRILY] I don't have it! I'm trying to get a full-time job. I'm two years (sic)!

I thought you were a lawyer.

Well, there's no jobs. Not when I [UNINTELLIGIBLE]. So I'm not in any position to help out right now. Sorry.

FRANK: Could you help us out with a donation?

Mary Collins (Appointed to Associate Minister of Defence by Muldoon in 1989): Ooooh.

As you know, he's incurring some substantial legal fees right now.

I'm not really in a position to do that. I don't have any resources myself, you know. I'm not someone who has any independent means, at all. I work from pay-cheque to pay-cheque [at the BC Health Federation].

So it's not – I'd have to think about it, quite honestly. I'm just, financially, not in a position to be able to do very much.

Okay. Sure.

I mean, what were the expectations?

Well, according to his means, I suppose.

I think there are people who are a lot better off than I am, who would be more appropriate, quite honestly. I don't know.

FRANK: We have a list of 200 friends and colleagues that we're calling on. We were wondering if you could help us out.

Doug Bassett (Baton Broadcasting supremo and Muldoon chum): Well, I don't know you. I don't talk about Brian Mulroney with anyone I don't know personally.

I realize that.

I understand but I'm not going to deal with something like this over the telephone.

Bill Winegard (Appointed Minister of Science by Muldoon in 1989): I'm sure if he wins, he's going to collect his legal fees and all.

Yes, but it's the short term that's the problem. This could drag on for a very long time. Mr. Mulroney has given so much to the party, and we don't want to see him bled dry by this.

I appreciate that. My only question is that Brian's got about a thousand times more money than I have. Being realistic. Obviously, if the man lost, we would be prepared to come. But he's got more money to finance his interim things than I have.

Right.

He probably makes more in a month than I make in a year. However, if by chance – if you're really stuck – I could find a couple hundred bucks, but that's my limit.

Okay. Why don't I put you down as a "maybe" and we'll call you back.

Okay.

FRANK: Is there any possibility you could help with a donation?

Alan Gottlieb (Appointed Ambassador to the U.S. by Muldoon): Why don't you give me your phone number and I'll consider it and contact you.

Well, you could send a cheque directly to the law firm, Roger Tassé.

Was he with Lang Mitchener?

Yes, he used to be.

How much are you trying to raise?

Initially, maybe as much as $500,000.

But one doesn't know if he is going to be charged?

No, not yet. But he has already incurred a fair amount of legal fees just from the suit against the Department of Justice.

All right. I'll consider it and be in touch. [Gotlieb never calls back]

(July 17, 1996)
FRANK recruits centrefolds for Cosmopolitan's Canadian Edition

The Hunks of the North

All this talk about Cosmopolitan *bringing back their male centrefold – remember Burt Reynolds airing out his pelt in '72? – had us wondering which, if any, CanCon celebs would get naked if asked to appear in the magazine.*

With Canadian Bonnie Fuller now installed as Helen Gurley Brown's successor atop the Cosmo *masthead, it seems only reasonable that the trashy women's mag would go trolling for skank north of the border.*

Armed with this lame justification, FRANK posed as a Cosmo *researcher and phoned up a handful of homegrown personalities to ask if they would consider appearing in the buff for our Hunks of the North centrefold feature.*

Here's how it went . . .

FRANK: I'm calling from *Cosmopolitan* magazine, the Canadian edition. We are preparing for our fall launch in Canada and we'd like to find attractive, prominent Canadian personalities to launch the Canadian centrefold feature. And we'd like to include all different kinds of men.

Ernst Zundel (Holocaust denier): Dressed this time?
Well, that's not what we're thinking. Have you ever modeled in the nude?
No, never in the nude. I'm a very modest type. Besides, I am non-circumcised. And these days, the fashion business says men should be circumcised.

Well, these days, yeah. They tend to be. How would you describe your physical condition.
I'm flabby. I'm bald, potbellied and flabby.
Do you have any objection to posing in the nude at all?
Only if it's done tastefully.

Mark Breslin (Yuk Yuk's supremo): I don't think nudity is my strongest attribute. My big mouth is my strongest attribute. You want hunks, don't you?
FRANK: No. That's the whole point. We're looking for intellectuals, funny…
Well, okay, look, I'm in my mid-40s, I still have my hair, I'm not particularly lined, I'm not a muscular guy, I don't go to the gym, I'm not outdoorsy. And that will show in a photograph. So again, if you're talking about me wearing a pair of shorts and a sort of ripped up Oxford shirt, you know, that's sort of only open with one button down to the navel with the sleeves rolled up, that could work.

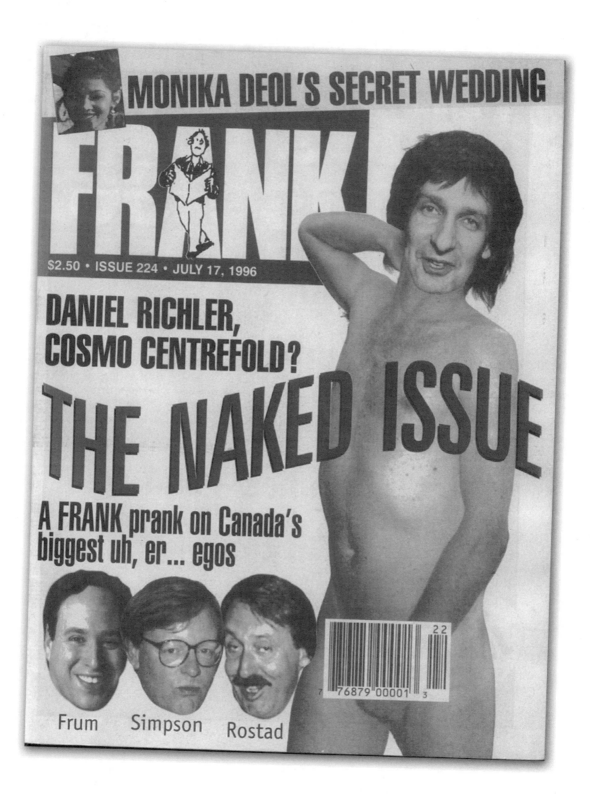

Do you mind me asking your marital status?

I'm single, straight, and 44. And I am considered somewhat of a catch. I'm a serial dater. I'm a swinging bachelor, sixties style. So in that way, you're on the right track. But I'm also 5'3".

Do you have any hobbies?

I'm the antithesis of an outdoorsy guy. I'm a theatre guy, I'm in night clubs all the time, fancy clothes, almost a boulevardier.

FRANK: You certainly have some qualities that would appeal to our *Cosmo* readers. Do you agree?

Claire Hoy (*Face Off* host): I don't know. What qualities are you looking for?

Someone who's distinguished. Someone who has a sense of humour as well as a certain charisma and smarts. Have you ever done any modeling before?

No. No.

Can you describe your physical condition? . . . Are you in good shape?

Well, I guess I'm just your average guy. Fifty-five-year-old guy.

Have you ever posed nude before? Even for fun?

No!

We certainly make our models look as good as they want to. You know we have an airbrush . . .

I don't think that kind of stuff's for me.

Mike Anscombe (Global-TV bingo caller): You know what? I've got to be honest with you. I don't think that I've ever seen *Cosmo* magazine. If I have, it would have been in the doctor's office. I didn't even know it was full-frontal nudity.

FRANK: We're thinking of bringing it back.

I just wouldn't do it with my profession and career. But that's just me. Maybe it's just my Quaker origins. As long as my mother's still alive I wouldn't.

And you're not into that.

I'm not. And I wouldn't use the word cheap because I don't consider it cheap. And I haven't even talked to my boss. I know Burt Reynolds thought it was funny and tongue in cheek but there's a certain persona where that would probably reinforce that persona. I'd have a hard time explaining this to Mom.

I understand.

Well, anyway, you know my decision: One, the boss would say no. And I could care less whether he would say no or not because it would be my decision. But if you were going to do something where one would remain clothed – and I'm not trying to suggest that you would do anything other than what you've done – then it would take a different dynamic.

Do you have any scars or embarrassing birthmarks?

I think any man who doesn't have a scar has never

been around. Anyway, maybe they'll decide naked is not the best way to go. And if they do, you have my number.

Wayne Rostad (*On the Road Again* host): Centrefold? My antenna goes "bringgg." How do you mean?

FRANK: It's a 3-page glossy. You open it up and it will have a bio.

And what am I doing? Am I languishing on a beach?

It's all up to you.

Oh. Okay. I could be standing in a barnyard with a horse.

We wanted first to ask you if you had any objections to full frontal nudity.

Do I have any objections to it? Yeah. I think so. I'm sure you'll find that most broadcasters or television type people would, obviously, decline the notion. I mean, to see Lloyd Robertson full frontal nude would certainly give me a different impression of Lloyd Robertson the next time I saw him on TV.

Well, let me ask you this. Have you done any modeling work before?

Not modeling, per se, other than the fact that I do a lot of stage work and I do a lot of photo sessions for our television show. I pose a lot for the camera. I'm not into the sexy image other than maybe a wholesome image or a healthy image. So, I'm

more inclined towards health and wholesomeness and country living and good living so the centrefold could be anything from the fact that I fly airplanes to I like my horses or just having fun jumping in the air – exhilaration. Zest for life. Zeal. Right.

It could be a warm photo close-up shot. It could be a smile, twinkle in the eye, it could be fun, it could be a laugh. See, I could capture in a centrefold something that is meaningful and warm and endearing if you capture it at the right moment and probably endearing and fun to look at.

How's your physical condition?

I'm in average condition for a – considering that I don't do aerobics every day. And I should. I mean, I could use muscle toning like anybody. But I have no concerns about my body. I feel quite good about it.

Do you have any scars or visible birthmarks?

No. Nothing like that.

We certainly do have quite a good photographer working with us. With a great airbrush.

Well, if my nose bothers you we can get that wart out.

What sorts of qualities do you have that would be appealing to women reading our magazine?

I think lifestyle is probably – anyone who has a hankering for rural living and some of the freedoms of living in the country. Certainly, if the weight of the trappings of the high-rise condominiums and the underground parking garage . . . I mean we're talking creeks on the property with lily pads on the water and we're talking hay in the fields and horses grazing and all those things. It has an appeal, of course.

Well, you sound like you'd be perfect for our "Hunks of the North" feature.

Hunks of the North? God love ya.

Well, for whatever it's worth, I'm 6'4", 240 pounds, I'm 48 years old, basically that's it.

Ian Brown (*Sunday Morning* host): Clothed or unclothed?
FRANK: We're tossing both around.

I think my boss would die. He'd just keel over. I'm just not the, uh, I'm not the, uh, well let me think about it. If that's okay.

What qualities do you think you have that would appeal to our readers?

I read a lot, I'm a good talker. I'm curious. I like sex.

What qualities do you find most appealing in women?

Brains, level of comfort with their body. It doesn't have to be a classic body but they have to be enthusiastic about it. This is off the record, isn't it?

Yes. We're just babbling.

Well, sense of humour is a good thing. Someone who understands an ironic joke and is capable of having at least two conflicting ideas in their mind at the same time without having a nervous breakdown.

And your marital status?

Definitely married. Just had a baby.

And how's your physical condition?

Not bad. Not bad. That's why I said I don't know if I'm your guy. But I thought I'd think about it. Because my inclination would be to say no, but that's such a stodgy predictable thing to do. Maybe it's better to think about it first. But I wouldn't have called myself

Playmate material.

Do you have any scars?

I have a broken nose.

You broke your nose?

Once when I was a boy and the second time when I was boxing. It can't be repaired. It's permanently scarred.

We want to know what you think your best qualities are, or those qualities that would be most appealing to women.

Ken Whyte (*Saturday Night* editor): I don't know your readers well enough. What are we looking at here?

We're looking at young to middle-aged women, professionals, who enjoy looking at all kinds of men.

Oh, God. I have no idea. I don't do

much but work so – is that attractive?

Sure is. What qualities do you find appealing in women?

I've been married for so long I don't even think about these things. I'm not going to be of any help to you at all. Women, mature women. Definitely. Grown up. And I work mostly with women. Most of the people at *Saturday Night* are women. Most of the editors are women, a lot of the writers are women. I'm surrounded by women. I'm married. I have one child. She's a daughter. So there's no getting away from them.

We're trying to look at men that are, well I wouldn't say ordinary, but less . . .

I'm so ordinary nobody would open the magazine.

Well, we believe that if we put your name on the cover as a teaser people will open it up.

Yeah? Well, that's a really interesting idea.

Do you have any objections to full frontal nudity?

Well, yes I do have objections. I'm really not the person you'd want for that. I don't think you have any idea how much you're flattering me.

Jeff Simpson (*Globe* windbag): I don't think I'm your target audience.

That's good. Because we're not trying to target you as an audience. We're looking for journalists, actors, all types to feature in our new centrefold series.

Sounds bad.

Your name came up in a meeting and we were wondering if you would be interested in helping us out.

Well, I'm afraid my ignorance is total. I don't know what your centrefold profiles are. I assume I get to keep my clothes on.

Well, that's something we're tossing around.

Not with me you're not.

We're wondering if you've done any modeling work.

No. Christ, no. Nor would I be remotely interested. I don't sell myself, God help me, on that sort of basis.

So you're a word man?

I'm a word man, I'm afraid. Very dull as a consequence.

Is that right. Have you ever posed before in your life?

Oh, of course. For cover shots and things like that.

Not in the nude?

Oh, Christ, no. Nor would I even consider it.

Steve Paikin (TVO host): Oh my God! Not like the Burt Reynolds centrefold!

Now we're bringing it back, but in a more sophisticated way. And we want to include all types of men.

Oh my God!

It's true. Have you ever done any modeling work?

No. Never, no. I'm just a boring guy from Hamilton. I think I'd get fired if I did it. Remember Peter Kormos did a Sunshine Boy thing with his clothes on and he got fired for doing it?

Actually, I wouldn't get fired, I'd be killed. They would slit my wrists for me.

Do you have any objections to full frontal nudity anyway?

No, I don't care. But I certainly have objections to showing my own body.

Oh, my God. Nobody wants to see that anyway.

You've never done any modeling work?

Absolutely not. I'm just a boring guy from Hamilton.

We do have quiet a good photographer.

Yeah, he'd have to be. Do you know who the sports editor of the *Globe* is?

No.

Dave Langford. Dave Langford is a very handsome, probably 40-year-old guy. I think he's single which would probably make this even better. Because, I'm like – did I mention I'm a boring guy from Hamilton?

Too often.

You don't want me. But you might want him. He's single, he's handsome, he's got a good job, he's an interesting fella, and I play baseball with him on Sunday so I checked him out lately and he's in very good physical condition.

You checked him out?

Well, he was wearing short pants. I couldn't help but notice. Maybe you should give him a shout.

I hope you're familiar with the magazine.

Dave Langford (*Globe* sports editor): Sure I am. Helen Gurley. I'd love to meet Helen Gurley Brown sometime. I know she's not with you anymore.

What do you look for in a woman? Similar qualities or someone to complement you?

Complement.

Absolutely.

Complement.

You've gotta have the initial attraction. To look across the room and say "wow, this woman is interesting" and then very quickly get the match-up of wits and brains and stuff like that. Whether you can sustain discussion and stuff like that . . .

Do you mind me asking about your marital status?

Single. That's why I'm good at this.

And do you have any hobbies besides sports?

As soon as you say sports editor of the *Globe* people just want to talk sports and I don't particularly like sports. I have a real passion for baseball but the rest, you know, I'm not going to sit at home all night and watch Hockey Night in Canada ever.

Well, that's attractive to a woman.

I'd much rather go to the Royal Alex or something like that. You've gotta make sure sports isn't your whole life. But you know, I work out, I have seasons tickets to the Jays, go to dinner, go to the theatre, go to movies.

How would you describe your physical condition?

I work out 4 or 5 times a week at the SkyDome fitness club. I'm in good shape. People would say I am in good shape.

Would you ever object to modeling for us? The reason I'm asking is we're thinking of bringing back the male centrefold.

Oohhh. Oooooh. Ohhhh. Hmmmmm. Yikes. I'd have to think about that one.

Do you have any objections to full frontal nudity?

Oh, yeah. The *Globe* would go crazy. I do object.

Now I have to tell you first of all, Steve Paiken advised me to call you.

Oh, yeah. I play ball with Steve on Sundays. Did he agree to it?

He tossed it around a while but I believe he has employer concerns as well.

Well, let's have lunch or something and talk about it.

Daniel Richler (former VJ): **I actually did a series of photographs stripped to the waist in a kind of send up of hip hop fashion, for CBC *Newsworld*, that they never used. It was a little over the top. I think it was a little too aggressive for them. It was amusing. It was fantastic.**

Like a fashion thing?

Yeah. Like a kooky fashion spread. It was supposed to defy the stereotypical *Newsworld* television host and so I could find it for you.

How would you describe your qualities that are most appealing to women?

I don't know. I know why I like women.

Why do you like women?

Because they're better company than men. When I was more identified with rock and roll television, perhaps it was appealing to be sort of a charming rebel, akin to the Beatles, sort of. On the edge but not too threatening. Maybe that's what people like.

David Frum (*Financial Post* columnist): **Well, I'm not attractive is the problem.**

FRANK: Well, as I said, we're looking for all different kinds of men.

Sure, that would be fine, but as I say it's not going to make for a handsome photograph.

Well, we do have a fairly good photographer.

Well, before I agree to this, I know *Cosmopolitan* USA has kind of a – has an interest in kind of intimate matters. I don't usually talk in public about things like that.

Well, that's the thing. We're trying to get the more intimate side of our candidates. For instance, what qualities do you think you have that would appeal to our *Cosmo* readers?

I think maybe we should take this from the top. I would find it very awkward to list what my good qualities are. I spend most of my mental

time thinking about my bad qualities anyway.

What qualities do you find in yourself that you feel would appeal most to women?

Michael Coren (CFRB loudmouth): There are certain characteristics I take very high, such as faithfulness and loyalty and I take my marriage very seriously. When I was younger, of course, you'd go out with a lot of different girls and so on. But I don't think I've ever two-timed anyone even when I didn't think it was going to be a very long relationship.

As far as the magazine goes, we'd like to get you into the studio, we've got quite a good photographer and we want to take some pictures. How would you describe your physical condition?

I'm in pretty good shape, really, because I play a lot of soccer, but what sort of things would you like me to do?

Well, we were thinking of doing something a little more racy.

Hmm. I don't know about that because I have sort of a persona. So what were you thinking of?

Well, we're running it by some of the men we're contacting, if they'd want to do any partial nudity.

I don't mind doing a thing a bit fun like appearing, say, in a complete soccer kit or something. That would be quite fun because I have any number of soccer kits to wear. So that sort of thing, sure. I don't mind doing that. Who are the people you're thinking of?

John Haslett Cuff, Ralph Benmergui, Ian Brown . . . Rick Salutin.

Ugh. Rick you might have trouble with. Ian, he's a nice guy, and Ralph, but Rick can be very lugubrious and touchy. But you know he might be willing to do this. I'm not sure.

(October 9, 1996)
Preston Manning's Makeover

With Preston Manning forced to defend his new haircut in the House of Commons, FRANK went into damage-control mode on behalf of our Reform friends. Posing as a braunshirt from Manning's office, we called up several Ottawa-area hairdressers and asked if they could repair Presto's hair. Here's how it went . . . .

FRANK: I'm calling from the office of the Leader of the Reform Party. We're looking for someone to come in and cut Mr. Manning's hair.

Mario (Hair Studio): Where would they have to go?

Well, it would be up here on the Hill. The Parliament Buildings.

What facility would you have there?

Nothing really. You'd have to bring your own equipment.

You would just have a room?

Yes, a private office. I'm sure we could get some scissors if we had to.

Oh, no, no, no. no. Equipment is no problem. We have it. We've been around.

What do you think would be the best cut for him?

Hmm. Now I think he has it combed back. His hair is very short on the sides. At this stage, it wouldn't be very much, a very slight adjustment. He would need something more balancing.

More balancing? Like a duck-tail?

Well, his hair now is very short on the sides, but a little too much volume on the top. So we would have to take some volume on the top, so it would balance.

What about sort of a George Clooney look? Do you think that would work?

Yeah, that would work. It would need a little bit more time for the hair to grow, though. His first cut would be more of a balancing thing. His next you would see the difference. Now he seems to be too much to the extreme.

Yeah, no kidding. What would the charge be, Mario?

I'm sure we can work something out.

Ballpark — are we talking, like, a $100?

No, it wouldn't be that much.

THE COLLENETTE   THE CLOONEY

Liz (First Choice Haircutters): To be honest with you, I would get rid of that puffiness on top.
FRANK: Puffiness?
More of a natural looking — I'm talking quiet as a mouse here because there's people around.
I appreciate you being discreet. As you know, there's been some media attention.
I understand. I don't know if you remember Secretary of State James Baker. I did his wife when they came to Moscow.
You lived in Moscow? Do you have security clearance?
Yeah. I did. For her.
What did you do for her? She had a kind of beehive thing?
Yeah, right. I just washed it, and styled it, and that was it. I had all the security around. It was behind closed doors.
You were saying about the puffiness . . .
I would try to eliminate that. It's too yuppie. Is that the right word? In politics, I think he should be more like a lot of the military men, more basic but it's still got some style. I'm not talking old army stuff.

You're talking sort of a David Schwimmer kind of look?
Yeah, kinda. His haircut before, there was nothing wrong with it. Why did he cut it like that?
It was a stylist out of town. How long would this take?
It would probably take me like 15 or 20 minutes.
That's fast. What would be the charge?
I would just charge him what we charge, like $10.50. Well, $11.24 with tax.
I think we have a GST exemption number.
Oh, okay. [SOTTO VOCE] I'll talk to my boss, my immediate boss, and we may not have to charge.
No, we can't do that. We have to pay. Otherwise it looks bad.
Oh.
You may not get a very good tip, though.
Okay.

Debbie (Hair Cut 100): You can use some clipper work. You can use scissor-on-comb, which is a barbering technique. We would have to wash it

down. Clippers is the fastest way. It's pretty simple.
FRANK: We would want a different look.
Really? That's terrible. I think [the current cut] looks much better on him. It's not as poofy on the sides. It looks great, but I can see it's a little too trendy for the approach he's trying to get across.
We were thinking a George Clooney look. Would that be too much?
Uh, I think so. With the George Clooney look, it's forward in the front. He could do that — would he want to?
I don't know. How do you think it would it look?
He'd look studious.
I was thinking — that fellow General Boyle, with the Somalia Inquiry . . .
Yes, it's tapered. It's a little bit longer than military. It's quite a nice look. The only difference with his haircut and General Boyle's is that it's not blended in as much.
Okay.

THE TRAINSPOTTER

THE EARLY GRETZKY

THE DORKY, ACTUAL UNRETOUCHED PHOTO

FRANK PRANKS

Hair Cut 100—are you affiliated with the musical group in any way?

No, well, no. I got the name from it 'cause I like the sound of it. They only lasted a year.

Do you have any security clearance?

No. I'm bondable. I've never been in jail and I don't have a criminal record or anything like that.

Have you ever been a member of the Communist Party?

No.

Selina (Salon Mancini): My room-mate worked on the Hill. I helped out with haircuts.

FRANK: Oh, whose?

When Bob Corbett was on the Hill I used to do his hair.

What would you do with Mr. Manning's hair?

He probably doesn't want anything different. When you go for a big change, people stop recognizing you and it gets in the paper.

We're open to suggestions. Could you do a Bob Dole look? Sort of a short back and sides?

Yes, something clean and neat.

How about a David Schwimmer look? Do you think that would work for him?

I don't think so. It's also kind of . . . out. I hope you don't have it.

No. What's in?

People are just keeping with short and clean and more conservative. Or else really messy. Sticking up.

Could you do that for him?

I can't see him wearing it.

John (Art Hair Coiffure Unisex): I would have to study what he has. Basically, advise as to what should or should not be done. Therefore, if it complied to what I said or his input as well, repair whatever had been done.

Um . . . Okay. We want sort of a new look for him.

Away from the traditional. I do Beryl Gaffney's. Unfortunately, she hasn't been in for awhile.

We wouldn't want anything like that.

No. You want more of an update. Something a little bit shorter.

You think shorter? Like a 90210 sort of thing?

Well, not quite. The man is a little older than that. Yeah, basically on that line.

Something that might appeal to the younger voters.

Yes, exactly. Something like the Clooney cut . . .

The Clooney! Sort of the Spartacus thing?

Yes. Forward, but a little bit more tousled. Especially if he's out there conversing with the people and what have you. It really doesn't matter if the wind blows through it or not. Right now, it would be almost like the René Lévesque in reverse. You want something that you just put your hands through and put back in place.

We wouldn't want a Réne Lévesque look for him. That would be wrong for him.

We couldn't achieve that unless we shaved him on top.

FRANK: We were thinking of something a little more modern.

Eli (Gilio Unisex & Hair Styling): Maybe a little bit longer on the top, a bit longer with more layering so it feathers back.

Sort of a Wayne Gretzky thing?

No, no.

What are the kids wearing today?

Kids? I don't know if you want a haircut like a kid, shaved on the side and punkier on the top.

No, we don't want anything punk. But maybe something the movie people are wearing. You know that movie *Trainspotting*?

[LONG PAUSE] For him? I have only seen him on TV so I don't know what kind of personality he is. Sometimes make-up can change a person quite a bit.

Make-up? We don't want to make him look like a homo.

Oh, no, no. You know what I mean — when you put make-up on for TV.

You mentioned perms and colouring.

That's what I'm thinking. Either a perm or a soft-colour. Maybe a soft highlight. I'd have to see how he looks. I do some people on TV myself. I don't know if you've ever heard of [local CBC bingo caller] Trish Macdonald?

Trish Macdonald?! What does she get done?

I give her highlights, sometimes perms.

She's not a natural blonde is what you're saying.

Oh, no, no. And Ken Macdonald I do. He's her brother. He's on Global, actually. He covers Parliament Hill.

What do you do for him?

I cut his hair.

Cover up that bald spot?

No. He's not bald. Lots of hair.

Dandruff?

No. He looks good.

FRANK: We're looking for someone to come up here on the Hill and cut Mr. Manning's hair.

Elie (Elie's Hairstylists): We don't do that.

You don't do men's hair?

No. We don't go out to do haircuts.

Even for Mr. Manning?

[LONG PAUSE]

This is for Preston Manning.

I don't know who that is.

He's the leader of the Reform Party.

[ANOTHER LONG PAUSE]

You don't know who that is?

Sorry.

(January 15, 1997)

A FRANK prank recasts CBC's hit comedy, The Newsroom.

For God's Sake, Elwy, Come Down!

The penultimate celebrity status symbol for Toronto TV, media, and entertainment wanks is a chance to make guest appearance playing themselves on CBC's The Newsroom. *The show has already featured ego-asserting cameos from John Haslett Cuff, Daniel Richler, Linda McQuaig, and a host of other Hogtown snoots. Posing as* Newsroom *creator Ken Finkleman's casting assistant, we called up a few more walk-on wannabes and invited them to appear in the following scenarios.*

FRANK: I'm calling from the comedy show, *The Newsroom*. We're kicking around some ideas for some new scripts and you know we have Canadian celebrities do cameos on the show. We were wondering if Mr. Robertson will be interested in making an appearance on the show.

Collette Wright (flak for Lloyd Robertson): Well Lloyd's away right now. . . .

Do you want to hear the idea we have?

Yeah. Sure.

As you know, he's considered Canada's most trusted newscaster. Anyway, we want to bring him in to replace our newscaster on the show. But they're worried about his health. He shows up and he keeps forgetting names and we have to keep reminding him why he's there. He calls every one Betty. And finally he wanders off and later he' found in a stairwell.

Oh, my God. I don't think he's gonna

go for something like that.

No? You don't think so?

Well, I mean that's up to him. Well, I think if you write that down he'll look at the idea and he decides that kind of stuff, you know. But I'll definitely put in his hands.

FRANK: We were wondering if Mr. Berton would be interested in making an appearance on one of our shows.

Elsa Franklin (PR flack for Pierre Berton): I'm sure he'd be de-lighted. He loves the show. Oh, yeah.

Ken Finkleman

He'd be tickled pink.

FRANK: We were tossing around some ideas, actually. One of them is kind of racy and I want to run it by you. He comes into the offices of the newsroom and he comes into the cafeteria and runs into one of the women working there and she's an older woman and she used to . . .

He's 76.

Yes, she's quite a bit older. And she used to be one of the Sordsman's playmates. . . .

No. Forget it.

No?

No. Because there is no Sordsman playmate.

No?

No.

FRANK: Well, let me tell you the plot scenario, first of all, that we're thinking of for Farley Mowat. We're kind of trying to use an event that's happened already that people are savvy of or aware of.

Dara Rowland (agent for Mowat): Oh, yeah.

So, he shows up with Ken Finkleman, who's our news director, at a luncheon. Later an anecdote from Finkleman's speech turns up almost verbatim in an article of Mowat's for *Canadian Living* where he claims it happened to him.

Plagiarism.

Yes. And Finkleman is outraged but you know he's always kissing up to everybody. He still sucks up to Mr. Mowat and compliments him on his writing.

Yeah. Well, just off – I cannot speak for Farley – but off the top of my head, this is obviously the *Saturday Night* piece and off the top of my head, I don't think he would want –

FRANK: Mr. Finkleman was tossing around some new ideas for the show and you know that we like to get local celebrities in to do guest appearances. And we were hoping you would be interested in making an appearance on the show.

Elwy Yost: Well, it would mean coming to Toronto?

Yeah. And we would take care of the expenses.

If there's something you want me to do, and I trust there's a little fee with it, then sure. I'm sure there would be something I could do.

We've got some ideas we were hoping we could send to you. One of them is a little more risqué than the others so I might just read it to you now . . .

A little what?

Risqué, perhaps.

Rescale?

Risqué. A little more racy. What we have in mind is, you're suffering a breakdown after too many viewings of King Kong. . . .

Ha. Ha. I love that.

. . . You strip. And you climb to the top of the Empire Club building. And you're talked down by the newsroom anchor Jim Walcott. He's forced to impersonate Vincent Minelli to get you down.

Vincent Minelli?

Why Vincent Minelli?

Because he's so often on your show.

Oh. Vincent Minelli. He's dead now, right?

Yeah.

But that doesn't matter, does it?

Well, you've already gone bonkers.

Oh, God. Now, listen, how would that be shot? 'Cause I can't stand heights as a person.

Well, you wouldn't actually be on top of the Empire Club. You'd be in a studio.

Thank God.

But it would require a butt shot to get you down.

Oh, God. Well, that sounds good.
[AFTER SOME CHATTER ABOUT EXCHANGING FAX NUMBERS, YOST'S WIFE GETS ON THE PHONE]

Mrs. Elwy: My husband says I should find out what the weather's been like in Toronto.

It's terrible, Mrs. Yost. It's snowing.

It's snowing? Oh, I like snow. I like snow.

FRANK: We were wondering if you'd like to make an appearance.

Phil Mathias: I suppose that would be fine. Can I give you an answer in 24 hours?

We had a suggestion from one of our writers and I was hoping I could run it by you. The way it goes is, you would be a longtime friend of Ken Finkleman, the news director.

Lloyd

That's almost true.

Oh, really?

Well, I know his brother Danny very well and I've met Ken. I don't know if Ken would remember me but I've met him in Danny's house.

Anyway, you would play his buddy and the two of you would go out for drinks in the local pub, or in the restaurant downstairs and you would disclose after a couple of drinks that the source of the English translation of the RCMP's letter to the Swiss was Mulroney himself. And Finkleman would be in conflict about whether to run the story.

Well, I understand *The Newsroom* is satire but I don't know whether that would be too close to the bone. I think it probably would. But I'll kick it around. My problem with that is people might believe it would be true.

(MATHIAS LATER CALLS BACK AND DECLINES OUR OFFER)

FRANK: Have you ever watched the show?

Vijay Patel (asst. to Jag Bhaduria): Eight o'clock morning? No.

It's not on at 8:00. It comes on Monday nights at 9:30. What we were thinking is Mr. Bhaduria would come in as himself, make a cameo. He would arrive in the newsroom and give his résumé to the director in the newsroom as if he were looking for work as a law reporter.

Yes . . .

And the résumé would say he was with ABC in Afghanistan, and CNN in Iraq, etcetera. But the résumé is obviously a fake because ABC is misspelled

"Still in Development":

Plot lines that we're waiting for a chance to pitch.

•**Ovide Mercredi**. A few minutes before a newsroom interview, Ovide says he's slipping out to buy cigarettes and will be back in five minutes. He doesn't return.

•**Donovan Bailey.** Opening a new mall, Donovan announces his conversion to the Nation of Islam and calls Oakville "Hymieville." Decides

rather than race Michael Johnson, he will lead the "Million Fastest Men March" on Ottawa. Finkleman undermines it, as he has block tickets for the race.

•**Steve Stavro.**
Finkleman is Stavro's guest at Leafs' game. The grocery magnate claims to love Leaf tradition, but once he breaks out the Ouzo, Stavro confides

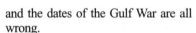

that the new arena will be called Knob Hill Gardens, and instead of players' names, Leafs' jerseys will now bear weekly produce specials (eg. Gilmour will be skating around with "Star-Kist Tuna $1.19/tin" on his back). Finkleman decides to sit on story because he believes in free enterprise and free tickets to games.

and the dates of the Gulf War are all wrong.
Hmmmm . . .
Anyway, the news director calls security and the next day Mr. Bhaduria sues the network for wrongful dismissal. And that's the story.
Okay . . . Well, I'm just surprised you would take a subject like this.
We all know it's tongue in cheek but it pokes fun at the troubles he's having now.
Okay, so we're looking at early February? I'll check and see if the dates are okay . . .

FRANK: Would you like to make a cameo appearance?
Brian D. Johnson: Oh, I'd be delighted. I love the show. Can I do a David Duchovny and be gay? No. Just joking.
Well, we havesome ideas. . . .

You're a film reviewer for *The Newsroom*. . . .
Yeah?
You come in, you're reviewing films, and they put you together, in a team, with Ed the Sock.
I like that. Yeah. That's good.
You're not happy –
No, I'm not happy with that. No, I mean Liz Braun's one thing, Ed the Sock is another thing.
Well, the thing is, you agree reluctantly. But you're not happy about it . . . anyway, on the first show, Ed calls himself Edward D. Sock.
[LAUGHTER]
. . . and he upstages you. He's much more knowledgeable, witty, bright, whatever. You're not happy about it. You're trying to get him dumped for Liz Braun.
Uh, yeah, okay.
But it doesn't work. So you quit, but before you quit you sneak into Ed's dressing room and shred him with garden shears.

FRANK PRANKS

FRANK lines up a celebrity slate of Tory candidates

Citizen Elwy Admits "I Inhaled"

With the Progressive Conservatives recruiting novelty candidates like Maj. Gen. Lew Mackenzie (ret'd.) to run in the next federal election, FRANK wonders just how low the party will sink to win votes.

Posing as a Tory fixer we called up a gaggle of candidates we'd like to see on the ballot and asked them to throw their hats in the ring.

FRANK: I'm with the candidate liaison office at PC Party headquarters.

Our election-readiness committee has been identifying some people we think might be good, possible candidates for us in the next federal election. Your name is one that came up.
Gino Empry (agent): I'd have to think about it.
Have you ever had any involvement in politics?
Well, yes, I was very much involved with Art Eggleton when he tried to become mayor and worked with him in the years he wasn't mayor.
Are you still involved with him?
No, not now. We're friends, but I'm not involved with him.

What kind of issues do you think voters would most strongly identify you with?
Probably entertainment, culture.
What skills do you have that would be valuable as a member of parliament?
Connections, speaking abilities, knowledge, the ability to see both sides.
Can you name the capital of New Brunswick?
Moncton . . . Fredericton.
Okay. Now, many of the Toronto ridings we have already filled, but we do have some openings in northern Manitoba.
Does that mean I'd have to go to northern Manitoba?
Well, you would have to, to run.
That might be interesting.
Ever do any hunting?
Not really.

The Front Benches: Jean Charest, Al Waxman, Mr. Dressup, Ziggy Loronc

TORY CANDIDATES

Michael Moriarty (actor) What is the PC Party? Progressive what?
FRANK: Progressive Conservative Party of Canada. We've been identifying people who might make good candidates.
You have to be Canadian, and I'm not Canadian.
Well, that's not entirely a problem. We can work around that. What would qualify you to be a member of parliament?
I don't know. The point is, my beef is with American politics. I admire the parliamentary system. It's not my aim to change Canadian politics.
Okay.
I'm not a big fan of Québec. If they want to secede, go ahead, that's my personal thing. Left, whining black organizations in the States – I come up here and find the same thing. Cultural despots, you know.
Uh-huh.
Don't regulate and force your culture down my throat, and then say it's still not enough. It's a song I heard down the in States from a large coalition of Afro-Americans who think we owe them a living.
Have you ever sought election to political office at any level.
No I came out for president of the United States, then I saw the elections laws and I couldn't work, so I withdrew. It lasted about 24 hours.
Is there anything in your personal history

Michael Moriarty

that might reflect badly on your candidacy?
Well, I'm outwardly honest. I do smoke and I do drink. When I was 23, I was unjustifiably put into a mental institution and given ten electric shock treatments.
Are you now, or have you ever been a member of the Communist Party?
No way, Jay!!!
What kind of issues would voters most strongly identify you with?
First Amendment, which is not a factor up here. Freedom of speech. And the criminal justice system.

Right. You were on a television program?
Yes, *Law & Order*. I played a prosecuting attorney in New York City.
What skills do you have that would be valuable as a member of parliament?
Eloquence, clarity of vision, integrity. I stick to my position. I respect others' positions, but it doesn't make me waver from mine. And I'm fiercely loyal to freedom, individual freedom.
Can you name the capital of New Brunswick?
Ah, now you've got me. I'm totally dead on the provincial capitals.

FRANK: We're really interested in bringing in new faces to the party.
Ernie Coombs ("Mr. Dressup"): Actually, it's the wrong party.
How's that?
I'm not a Conservative.
You're a Liberal?
I think so.
Oh, anything we could do to change your mind?
No, I think not.
As I say, we are broadening our perspective.
No. I'm – if anything – withdrawing from the public arena, as it were. I'm just doing live shows, speeches. I'm trying to wind down.

Margeret Kemper (former First Lady): This is the Progressive Conservatives?
FRANK: Yes.
And you know who I am?
You're Mrs. Margaret Kemper.
I used to be Margaret Trudeau.
You were previously married?
To the prime minister.
The prime minister?
Prime Minister Pierre Trudeau.

Gino

FRANK PRANKS

Oh, I didn't make the connection.

I would be a great person, other than that I would be laughed at. There's no question that I'm a strong supporter of change. I think Jean Charest has made wonderful steps with the Conservative Party and I would like to see them make a substantial gain in the next election.

The political spectrum has changed dramatically since you were married.

Oh, yeah. I actually haven't had any political involvement, having been so badly burned. Public life wasn't fun for me.

I will just zip through the standard questionnaire. Your age?

Forty-eight.

Marital status.

Married.

Bilingual?

Yes. Je pense pas plus [UNINTEL-LIGIBLE]

Is there anything in your personal history that might reflect badly on your candidacy?

[LAUGHS] Perhaps.

Do you use, or have you ever used non-prescription drugs?

Ah, yes. I have in the past. And I inhaled, too. So that probably eliminates me. I would think that you wouldn't find anyone who was relevant who hadn't, being our generation. Not that I do any more.

Any history of mental illness?

Uh, no. Perhaps nervous breakdowns, but nothing more. No, I've been accused of having had a nervous breakdown when I had enough. I think that was politically expedient to say I had a nervous breakdown.

What kinds of issues would voters most strongly identify with you?

Oh, women's issues. And issues about water.

Pardon me?

Water. Natural resources. Water as our primary natural resource that we have to be the careful stewards of.

Can you name the capital of New Brunswick?

Moncton?

No, it's Fredericton.

Fredericton? I was going to say Thurso.

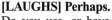

Maggie

Al Waxman (master thespian): I don't want to run for political office. I have been asked, and indeed by the PC Party, to take a diplomatic posting. I turned it down.

FRANK: Which posting was that?

The Counsul-General to Los Angeles. Ironically, Kim Campbell is now in it. She's excellent. The likelihood is that the next time I'm offered a diplomatic posting I will probably say yes. I am not of a mind to run. I've been asked by Mike Harris, and at the same time by Lyn McLeod, to run here in Ontario.

Okay. We were also discussing the possibility of a Senate posting. How would you feel about that?

Well, I'd be thrilled. I'm coming down there next week. I'm being invested in the Order of Canada. The Order's Latin motto, *desirontes meliorium patrium* – "they desire a better country" – I thought that was lovely and that's really where I'm at. I love Canada. I chose to focus here rather than take the invitations to go down to Los Angeles.

Maybe the Senate would be a good place for you.

Well, it's ironic. When certain people in the Liberal government were talking about a posting for me abroad, one of them said, "Why have him away? He should be here. He's Canada's ambassador to Canada."

Okay. I'm going to pass on your comments to the committee.

Don't make it sound like I'm lobbying. When I got the Order of Canada this week, so many letters came to me saying, "about time... overdue" and stuff like that. These things happen, forgive me, like wine. When it's the right year, it happens.

Perhaps it will be Senator Waxman in 1997.

That would be great.

Elwy Yost (TV host): Oh, Jesus. I don't know what to say. You've flabbergasted me. I always thought my name should be Citizen Yost.

FRANK: Mr. Charest himself thought you might . . .

I've voted both ways in my time. I've always been a great admirer of Bill Davis. But I've voted Liberal, too. I don't know what I am right now. This might help solve it.

It might.

I'd have to discover what's involved. I do my shows. I have to fly east.

Would you be interested in running in Vancouver or Ontario?

Well, I'm not known out here. I'm known in Ontario. I live out here. So, it could be expensive for me.

Well, the party could certainly help out with your expenses, in terms of campaign expenses. That wouldn't be a problem.

I might have to do a whole bunch of shows in there. They're damn demanding.

Well, we're flexible. We can work around that. Maybe you could work the campaign into your television program a little?

Oh, God, no. TVOntario wouldn't allow that. It would be nice, but I think . . . I would have to go through Herndorff and the rest of them. I suspect they keep their hands away from politics.

Now, if you were successful as a candidate, you would probably want to commute to Ottawa. You would be in the House 100 days a year. There's a good salary and pension plan.

Oh, God almighty! I've got to talk to my wife. This is so bewildering. Of course, I'm interested. For a character like myself, this is a really dramatic moment.

Have you ever sought election to political office at any level?

I have, through the years. It's sort of a very dramatic kind of thing. Some of my favourite films have been pictures like *Citizen Kane*, which gets involved in politics, and *The Great McGuinty*. I'm fascinated, though I've never been one to

Citizen Elwy

spend my life studying politics. I like to write fiction.

You're writing a book?

Yes, I have been for ten years. It keeps getting rejected. It's adventure and mystery, strange things. It's an exciting thriller, a search for a lost movie.

Are you now, or have you ever been, a member of the Communist Party?

Good God, no! I detest that whole left-wingism.

What issues would voters identify you with?

Well, they identify with seeing me and knowing me for 25 years and before that with the CBC. I did shows from 1959. So I've been a broadcaster for 39 years. I guess a man who is reasonably intelligent and warm. I'm supposed to be a very warm person.

Ever smoked marijuana?

Wait a minute – one night, years ago, my kids were young. Chris had some pot or something. I remember taking some one night. Once. I can still remember lying down. Chris sort of laughed and thought his dad was exploring this with him. It's interesting enough. I can remember lying on the sofa, some music was playing, and it was like great big balls – grapes – in the air. I went to sleep. That was the full extent of it? That's the only thing. I enjoy a drink.

Any drunk driving charges?

No, nothing like that. Just a second. [TO WIFE] Just a second, sweet. [UNINTELLIGIBLE] This isn't FRANK Magazine, is it?

Pardon?

FRANK Magazine? [Yost describes at length his appearances in past FRANK pranks.]

I don't actually read the magazine. It's sort of trashy.

Pardon me for asking that. I must tell you something amusing. One of

my favourite films is *The Treasure of the Sierra Madre*. **Do you know it?**

Humphrey Bogart.

Yes. At the end, the old man, Old Howard, he saves the life of an Indian and they're wondering what's going to happen to them. Bogart's dead at this time. Old Howard says, "They're going to make me their legislature." So, I've been using that.

I've always like, "Rifles?! We don't need no stinkin' rifles!"

No. badges. "We don't need no stinking badges." But very good, my friend, to come up with that.

Ziggy Lorenc: Oh, my God! That's wild. Ooooooh!

FRANK: Do you have any experience with politics?

Yes, I have, actually. When I was working with MuchMusic, in particular. I covered the PC Convention in Ottawa. So I had more knowledge once I covered that and spoke with Kim Campbell. I spoke with her maybe four times, four separate interviews.

Kim actually recommended your name.

My God, I'm sort of taken aback.

Would you be able to take 40 days off to run an election campaign?

That's very interesting. I would have to speak to the president of the station, Moses Znaimer. Then I can see what happens from there.

What issues would voters most strongly identify you with?

I think the feminist platform. Daycare. Big time.

What skills do you have that would be valuable to a member of parliament?

I guess my communication skills, number one. I read a lot. I'm big on literacy. I have a program dedicated to authors. Let me see. There's so many. In the entertainment world, I sing. I play the piano. I'm interested

in the arts. That's all I can think of at the moment.

Can you name the capital of New Brunswick?

Actually, you know what? I can't at the moment. I'm in shock. Sorry. I've been through there, too, which is interesting.

Yeah, it's Fredericton.

I know there are two St. John's out on the east coast.

That's right. The New Brunswick one has no "s".

That's it!

FRANK: If we were to offer you the Fitness and Amateur Sport portfolio . . . .

Rod Black (CTV Sportscaster): Oh, absolutely. I'm a person who believes strongly that it's screwed up in this country. It's obviously become the forgotten portfolio. I remember when Otto [Jelinek] was there, it seemed to have a better profile.

Do you know Otto?

Yeah, very well, actually.

He was the one who suggested your name.

Otto is a great man. We worked together at the Olympics.

Oh, the skating . . .

I tell ya what, there are a lot of out of shape, overweight kids who aren't doing a lot right now with their bodies and with their minds. They both work together.

Can you name the capital of New Brunswick?

St. John's.

There was something about a comment you made, about "pitch the bitch"?

That was a comment that wasn't even made by me. It was a *Globe and Mail* report that was erroneous and out of context. In skating, the skaters actually use that terminology. I said that to that reporter [Mary Jolimore] and it was put in print that I made it up. I probably could have won a lawsuit.

(June 4, 1997)

A FRANK-DECIMA RESEARCH POLL

Live, Willing Women Are Waiting For Your Hot Call; Plan to Back Liberal Slate

Phone-sex operators speak to hundreds of ordinary Canadians and perverts every week. Who better, then, to act as barometer of the prevailing political zeitgeist? FRANK called a handful of these hard-working gals, at rates starting as low as 69¢ a minute, to ask who they're backing on June 2.

LIVE FEMALES ONLY
1-613-976-5999

FRANK: Which party will you be supporting?

Brandi: I haven't decided. Well, to be honest with you, I got something interesting in the mail. And I was trying to decide what it was all about. Did you see something called the Canadian Action Party? CAP?

Uh, no. What do you think of Jean Chrétien as a leader?

Well, he's doing the best he can. But I don't think he's good enough. He promised no more tax, and he's put the taxes up higher and higher, so I don't have much faith in him.

Do you think Jean Charest would do a better job?

I don't think he would, either. I don't have faith in anybody in politics right now.

Which leader do you think best represents the interests of phone-sex workers?

I would just have to say Liberal, because they're liberal. That's all I can say from common knowledge. Liberals are supposed to be liberal about matters. Conservatives are more religious and they would be against it. But if they look at the statistics and they see the capacity of

our generation of men today and what they spend their dollars on in the adult entertainment services, it would be astronomical.

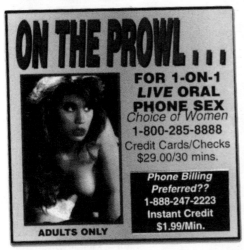

MOST GRAPHIC XXX
1-613-976-4225

Cynthia: I don't get involved. I'm not voting capacity in this country. I'm from the UK and I'd like to keep it that way, 'cause I've got British status.

FRANK: Are there any of the leaders who appeal to you?

Well, I guess we'll have to stick with the Liberal Party – Chrétien, the guy with the crooked face. The only reason I say that is because Trudeau was probably the best leader Canada has had and they can only try to follow in his footsteps. Of course, he got a bit sidetracked when his wife started running around with the Rolling Stones.

Sure. Right.

So he lost his credentials, didn't he? But I'd have to say we have to stick with the Liberal Party. If you shuffle around too much it will cost your country money.

What effect do you think Tony Blair's victory will have on the Canadian election?

Is he with the NDP?

MY ROOMMATES AND I WANT TO PLAY LIVE
1-613-976-6969

Kelly: I'm supporting the Liberals. I just feel they do what they need done. That's sufficient reason. Actually, there's not much talk of politics in the office.

FRANK: Which political leader best represents the interest of phone-sex operators?

None. They probably don't even think about us. I mean, how many people think about us?

Quite a lot, judging by the ads in the newspaper.

Actually, they probably don't even approve 'cause it's going to take one person to get screaming and get us off the line.

What do you think of Jean Charest?

I like him, but he's not my personal choice.

What about his haircut?

His haircut? I guess it suits him.

And Preston Manning?

I don't like Preston Manning's attitude. I think he's too pushy. He hasn't got enough spunk. He's too hard driving. I think you need someone who's lively. You need a woman.

What about Alexa?

[LONG PAUSE] I don't know anything about her. Why? What's your choice?

I have to remain neutral. Do you ever get any calls from prominent Canadians?

I'm sure we've had MPs call. But none that I could name.

XXX FANTASY SELECTIONS
1-613-976-1010

Naughty Natasha: I'd rather not answer those types of questions.

FRANK: Could I talk to somebody else there then?

No, you can't. They won't answer those type of questions. I'm their boss.

Oh, do we get our money back then?

No, you don't get your money back.

How come you're calling a phone service to talk about the Liberal Party?

I guess I'm just kinky. I'll talk about any of the parties. Which party do you support?

All of them.

All of them equally?

Yes.

That's fairly democratic of you.

I believe in equal treatment. I don't even vote. I think it's bullshit. I think everything is rigged.

Rigged?

Yeah. I don't believe in it. Our votes don't matter. They just care about the tax. They just want their money. We all get humiliated in the process.

Do you find, running a phone sex service, that you're encumbered by a lot of taxes?

Oh, we have to pay taxes. Work is work. Payroll taxes.

So, taxation is an issue for you, then.

Of course.

NEW LIVE ONE ON ONE
1-613-976-6060

Soo-Lin: Oooh. I don't think I know. I don't get involved in political situations.

FRANK: Why not?

Well, I don't understand it most of the time. My English is not so good. I have not been here in this country a long time.

Where are you from?

I'm from China. A long way away.

So, do you think you might be inclined to support the NDP, then?

Well, I'm waiting for my papers to come. Then I am able to vote. Then I will get involved and learn all the parties. It is different from my country.

Do you know Jan Wong?

No.

(July 2, 1997)

FRANK courts no-hope Liberals for cabinet posts

"Am I in the Running?"

A week before Jean Crouton announced his new cabinet, ministerial wannabes waited anxiously by their phones for that crucial summons from the Prime Minister's Office. Posing as an assistant to PMO Chief of Staff Eddie Goldenberg FRANK called up a handful of backbench MPs and hinted that they might be under consideration.

FRANK: I'm assisting Mr. Goldenberg with a few background checks.

Sarkis Assadourian: Who is Mr. Goldenberg?

Eddie Goldenberg. From the Prime Minister's Office.

Oh, yeah. Right. Sorry.

As you probably know, the new cabinet will be appointed next week. And I have to do some background screening before any announcement is made.

Am I in the running?

Well, I can't really discuss that. Are you currently involved in any litigation?

Well, there was litigation against me by a volunteer in the 1993 election. He claimed he was supposed to get a job. The courts didn't go for it. He was on legal aid. Legal aid cut off funding because there was no litigation. We went after him two or three times. I think he gave up because there was no case.

Okay. Given your qualifications, which cabinet portfolio do you think you would be best suited for?

To be frank, Immigration would be the thing. I also like small businesses. I think small business is the way to go for the future. That would be the thing. If it's going to be other minor positions, I would think

Assadourian

CANADA HOUSE OF COMMONS

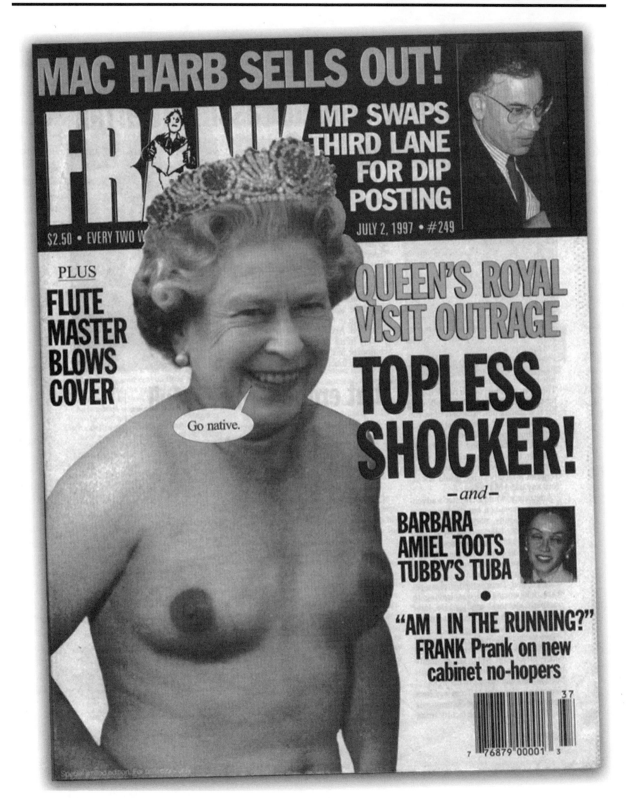

Multiculturalism probably, would be a valuable thing for me, I would appreciate. And the other is Foreign Affairs, I'm quite interested in Foreign Affairs.

Okay. Do you travel a lot?

Well, I don't travel. But I travelled in the past. I know quite a bit about history. Yeah, I like history, yeah.

Are you athletic, at all?

I used to play tennis and I used to play soccer. But that was when I was younger. I still play tennis once in a while.

I'm not saying anything by this, but let's just say there's an opening right now in Amateur Sport.

I would like to serve the government in whatever shape or form I can.

Okay. Are you currently involved in any sports right now?

I play tennis with my kids, as I said. And I don't smoke. I quit smoking July 1, 1989.

If this were to come up, do you think you could do a little training, get into shape for it?

Oh, yeah, I lost 25 lbs. on the campaign. I think Mr. Goldenberg will be getting in touch.

FRANK: Is there anything in your background that would disqualify you from a position in cabinet?

George Proud: Well, the only thing right now is that I've applied for protection. I got into a financial problem with two other people in a real estate deal. I didn't go bankrupt, but what I did, I gave notice – I did that to get through the election but it didn't do me any good because it all came out in the paper anyway – but what I've done is I gave notice that I would make a proposal to my creditors. We're going to

Proud

start working on it Tuesday and what I want to do is pay them off. But other than that, there's nothing that I know that would disqualify me. Chrétien knows about it.

Of course. Are you involved in any litigation?

I felt like doing it over the election, with the media. They were dragging this financial stuff of mine through the papers every day for 21 days they did it. The local paper.

Who were the reporters on it?

Doug Beasley and Barbara McKenna.

What's your relationship with them?

Oh, I don't like them, personally. They're slimebags, and I tell them that, and that doesn't help me either.

To which cabinet portfolio would you be best suited?

Oh, God. [LONG PAUSE] I don't know. Defence or Labour. Veterans Affairs. I was very much involved in that area.

How's your health?

Great. I exercise two hours every day in the gym. Weights and cardio. I done one day cardio.

You're on the Stairmaster.

Yup.

David Iftody: Gosh, I've spent quite a bit of time with aboriginal people. I've been a consultant with aboriginal people. I've been a consultant to Chief Billy Diamond, Assembly of First Nations, that sort of thing. I've a Master's in Public Administration. I guess in terms of economic development, western diversification, infrastructure development . . .

FRANK: Your answer doesn't

Iftody

have any bearing on anything . . .

Yeah, okay. My background is public management. Management consultant is my background.

Okay, I think PMO is pretty aware. How's your personal health?

I'm not – years ago, I was involved in sports and so on and aerobics. But in the last ten years, to be quite truthful, no. I just have the time to go to the weight room in Confederation once and awhile. But I'm not an all-star 10K runner. But if Jean Charest was appointed minister, I'm sure I could beat him.

Do you smoke?

No. Social drinker, don't smoke. Very outdoorsy. I'm a very outdoorsy kind of person.

FRANK: Are you currently involved in any litigation?

Tom Wappel: It's been settled. I sued my NDP opponent for libel. It's been settled to my satisfaction.

What was the substance of that?

They alleged that I wanted to set up concentration camps for refugees. This is, of course, ludicrously false. The case has been settled on the basis that he would issue a written apology, which he did, and that he would pay my legal costs, which he is doing.

For which cabinet portfolio would you be best suited?

Number one: Solicitor General. Number two: Immigration. I was the official opposition critic for the Liberal Party of Canada for Immigration and also Solicitor General. So, I know something about both departments.

Beth Phinney: One of the staff people had a lawsuit against me but it was dropped. She ended up having to pay me. The judge said it was

frivolous. She tried to blackmail me.
FRANK: For which cabinet portfolio would you best be suited?
I spent a lot of time in education, so it could be with youth. I'm a woman, whether that makes any difference for a woman's portfolio. I never think about it, then all of a sudden you're asked. You never think about what you're qualified to do.
Let me ask you, any military background in the family?
Yes, my dad was in the military, not very long. That's all. I'm in the Legion.
Oh, that's good.
I did them all a big favour. They were going to charge the GST on the memberships and I caught it when it was going through the House. Paul Martin pulled it at the last minute.
So you have a good relationship with the veterans community?
Yes, I've been working closely with wounded veterans coming back from Bosnia. I love anything Canadian. Just because I was in Guiding all of my life, my parents took me right across Canada a lot of times. I visited parks and that kind of thing interests me.
When you say Guiding...
Girl Guides. Scouting. All through leadership training. Right from being a little Brownie.
Well that's good because, entre nous, one of the areas where there is an opening is the veterans portfolio.
Well, that would be quite interesting. I would find that interesting.

I'm almost 60 myself, so it's not inappropriate even though I look young and I'm in good shape. I know it's not a big one. But I think it would be a good one for me to go into. It would be nice for a woman to do that.
Right. That's what we were thinking.
In fact if did didn't get anything, I was going to ask if I could be the parliamentary secretary to the Prime Minister so it would be a woman. I thought this would be a way he could have a woman going down the steps with him each day on Question Period.

FRANK: This is a matter of some sensitivity. I would appreciate it if you didn't discuss this with anyone else.
Dan McTeague: My wife is here. I'll go in the other room.
No, that's okay. These are boilerplate questions. Is there anything in your background that would disqualify you from a position in cabinet?
Not to my knowledge. No criminal record. No nothing. The only thing that came up in the campaign was the question of an error made by one of the staffers.
Which was that?
That was the issue of the Master's degree. This was sudden, instant discovery of a pre-election résumé. There were three of them; two were correct. The person in question, Heather Bird, tried to make a big issue out of it but it panned out.
That's the woman from the *Toronto Sun*? We've got a file on her.
I'd love to hear it some day. I went from 42 per cent to 53 per cent as a result of her attacks. It helped my election as opposed to hindering it.
Are you currently involved in any

litigation?
I wish I were.
With Heather Bird?
Yeah, exactly. There may be one pending with Chay Calabar. He perpetuated this thing about my Master's degree. I contemplated taking legal action during the campaign as a way to muzzle him. But it's only draft.
Have you ever been accused of sexual harassment by an employee or student?
No, not at all. Maybe my wife [CHUCKLE].
To which cabinet portfolio would you be best suited?
Any one involving some degree of bilingualism, youth. That would encompass Heritage, to a lesser degree Transport, any of the Secretaries of State.
Any familiarity with the issues involving Fisheries?
Um. No, none at all.
Do you do any fishing?
FRANK Magazine, right?
Pardon? I don't understand.
These questions have come out in the past. Ernie [Mr. Dressup] Coombs is one of my neighbours.

(October 8, 1997)
Gay Macaque Shoque!

Readers of the Ottawa Senior Citizen *were recently treated to a series of front-page stories about a group of research monkeys at Health Canada's Ottawa laboratories who were to be euthanized because of funding shortfalls. In the ensuing uproar from animal rights groups, the 115 monkeys were given a temporary reprieve.*

FRANK wondered if the austerity teachings of the Reform Party could be applied to save the monkeys from termination without blowing loads of taxpayer dough. Posing as a Reform researcher, we called up Health Canada's Chief veterinarian Dr. Pierre Thibert to give him a few suggestions. It went like this . . .

FRANK: I'm a researcher with the Reform Party here in Ottawa. The Leader's Office asked me to make some inquiries about the monkeys. I wonder if you could tell me what their status is.

Dr. Thibert: We used to breed monkeys for testing the vaccine of polio. There's no more requirement for polio testing, so therefore we're stuck with a major breeding program. And the use of animals in research – those animals at the ministry level, they put a hold on the issue.

Are these, like, apes?

No, no. These are – you know macaque?

Uh, no.

You know rhesus monkeys?

I know rhesus monkeys.

Okay, they are a small breed of rhesus. They come originally from

the Philippines, Malaysia, Vietnam. And what's the health condition? Some of them have AIDS?

They're excellent. Yes, some of them have AIDS.

These are, uh, homosexual monkeys?

No, no, no, no. AIDS is not only for homosexuals, you know.

How did they contract the AIDS, then?

They were injected, experimentally. They were injected with the Simian AIDS. In nature, monkeys harbour some similar viruses that are close to human AIDS.

You got any of those Ebola monkeys?

No, there has been Ebola in the States three or four years ago. Those animals came directly from the Philippines, from a specific supplier, and they destroyed all those animals.

I guess the costs for the government, then, is feeding them?

Yes, it's a major cost. But it has been distorted in reports. After twenty years of study, you want to extract all the data, and you want to proceed with necropsy.

One of the ideas for cost reduction our MPs were kicking around was the possibility of some kind of sponsorship from a food supplier, like a Chiquita Bananas or a Planters Peanuts – could they kick in?

I don't know about that. We really believe in trying to get corporate involvement in government projects. This seems like a natural, because of the humane element. It would save us some money.

Health Canada to kill 115 monkeys

BY CHRIS COBB
The Ottawa Citizen

Health Canada will begin killing about 115 monkeys next week, destroy-ing not only the animals but what

FRANK PRANKS

What do they eat?

They eat Monkey Chow.

Monkey Chow? Is that like Cat Chow?

Yes, exactly, it's made by Purina. There's enough monkeys in North America.

Really? Well, maybe Purina is something we could look at as a possible sponsor?

Yes, but for us to go and beg to Purina – it doesn't make sense. If we're not able to afford to feed our animals, we should be out of the business.

Could these monkeys be trained to do anything once they're finished their research, on a cost-recovering basis?

No, they're not social animals.

But they're pretty intelligent, right?

I'm not putting down the monkeys. You're right, they're intelligent. Naturally, they socialize with their colleagues and peers. But the purpose is to extract data out of them, not to retrain them.

We've had some calls from some fruit growers in our BC ridings who are wondering if they could be retrained to do some fruit picking.

No, they will eat the apples. They will destroy the tree.

How about filing or light industrial work?

No, monkeys in the wild – they are pests.

I've seen some monkeys that are sent up trees to bring down coconuts.

Yes, yes, yes.

I think those were gibbons.

But you say these monkeys are macaques?

Yes, exactly. Sure, they can be trained for certain things,

but not picking apples or whatever fruit crop. You will have the unions of the Okanagan Valley –

How about a petting zoo?

We have done so in the past, but again, these are experimental animals and we have to extract data. You want to study the liver, the brain.

Could those kind of studies be done – again, I'm thinking of costs here – on an outpatient basis? If you had some kind of adoption program, people could take them into their homes and pay for their feeding and such, then at specific times bring the monkey back for tests.

But people don't realize – a macaque is a vicious animal.

Vicious?

Yes, a macaque will bite you. A macaque will chew you. This is not a zoo. This is not a pet store. I am scientist. I want to study the brain. I want to extract the brain. I want to do a necropsy.

Oh, so you have to kill them anyway?

Exactly. They exaggerate this issue. It's not a question of feeding them.

You ever have any escapes?

No. Sometimes they escape from the cage and we catch them at room level.

So there's no chance there's any Ebola in these guys? You do any screening?

Yes, we do a screening. There's no Ebola. For sure.

(March 25, 1998)

Egoyan, Party of Four

For lesser members of the proletariat who want to dine at Toronto's top restaurants, reservations are often required weeks or months in advance. But it's a different story for the celebrity class. For them, a last minute phone call is all it takes to jump to the front of the queue.

To test film director Atom Egoyan's dinner clout, FRANK phoned some of Toronto's trendiest eateries and attempted to secure a table on his Oscar-nominated behalf.

We begin our calls at a reckless 6:00 p.m. on a Saturday night, a mere two hours before our intended arrival...

FRANK: Would you have a table for four at 8:00?

Rosewater Supper Club: Unfortunately, I don't. I can do a table for four early, around 6:30, or at 9:30.

It's for Atom Egoyan. Any chance you can squeeze him in at 8:00?

Yup. You just said the magic word. It's for four?

Yeah, and I don't know if you have something like this, but a table that's a bit more discreet?

Yeah, actually, I have a really nice booth in the back corner of the restaurant. Unless somebody was sitting right near them, they wouldn't know he was here. Would that be appropriate?

Yeah. Do you have non-dairy creamer?

I don't know. I'll check.

Atom Egoyan with the Missus.

Centro: Unfortunately, we're sold out until 9:30.

FRANK: It's for Atom Egoyan. Any chance you could squeeze him in?

Atom Egoyan? Hold on. [MANAGER COMES ON] Hello, may I help you?

Yeah, I'm trying to get a table for 8:00 for four.

We are booked up. Did you say it's for Atom Egoyan?

Yeah.

I just don't want him to have to wait. Let me see what I can do here.

He's with Mr. Jewison and Mr. Waxman.

Yes, that's fine. Oh, Mr. Jewison, too?

Yes, and Mr. Waxman. Mr. Waxman might be arriving early for appetizers.

Okay. See you then.

North 44: For this evening? We don't have nothing.

FRANK: It's for Atom Egoyan.

I'll have to check with my boss. Hold on. [LONG PAUSE] Sorry to keep you waiting. You're looking for four people for tonight?

Yes, for 8:00.

I could offer you 8:30 or 11:30.

No, the timing is sort of important. It's for Atom Egoyan.

Who?

Atom Egoyan, the film director.

Oh, the thing is, I can't have a table at 8:00.

He's dining with Mr. Redford and Mr. Jewison. It's an important meal.

Hmmm.

You know Mr. Egoyan is nominated for two Academy Awards? I think he's somebody you want in your restaurant tonight.

I'll see what I can do. It will be upper level though. I don't have anything in the main dining.

Let me reiterate: He's dining with Robert Redford!

I'll see what I can do for a nice table.

FRANK PRANKS

Avalon: I have something around 8:30.
Nothing at 8:00? It's for Atom Egoyan.
[LONG SIGH] All right, I'll take it.
Do you have a table that's discreet?
It's Saturday night. We're very busy. I'll do my best.
He's dining with Mr. Jewison.
I'll do my best.

Ellipses: We're completely booked tonight.
It's for Atom Egoyan. Any chance you can squeeze him in?
I wish we could. The earliest we could do is about 9:30.
Eeeek! The problem is he's dining with Mr. Jewison and Mr. Keitel. Is there any way that you can squeeze them in?
Hold on. [LONG PAUSE] We're going to do some creative juggling around.
Great.
Now, the entire restaurant is non-smoking tonight. Is that a problem?
Oooh, he likes to smoke American cigarettes. Could we just relax it around his table? I think Mr. Keitel likes to smoke cigars, too.
Okay, sure. We have a table that is sort of secluded back by the kitchen.
It's a good table, though?
Yes, it's a nice quiet spot.
What's the music like? You play background music?
A lot a different stuff. What's the preference?
Mr. Egoyan likes to bring a cassette of native folk songs.
We don't have a cassette player. We've only got CDs.
If he brought a CD, would that be okay?
Sure.

Winston's: Oh, I'm sorry, we can't. We're fully booked up. The only thing we have available is around 6:30.
FRANK: It's for Atom Egoyan. Is there any chance . . .
Who?
Atom Egoyan.
Who's that?
The film director. He's nominated for two Academy Awards. You don't know Atom Egoyan?!
No.
Is there any chance you squeeze him in at 8:00?
Hold on. [LONG PAUSE] Hi, we're just checking the tables for you.
Okay. He's dining with Mr. Jewison and Mr. Keitel, so it's sort of an important meal.
They're in the movie business?
Mr. Egoyan is a film director. Mr. Keitel is an actor and Mr. Jewison is also a director.

Hold on. [LONG PAUSE] Hi, I'm going to try to squeeze you in. The name again?
Egoyan. E-G-O-Y-A-N.
E-G-O-Y . . . ?
. . . A-N.
Okay. I'll put you somewhere nice.

(June 17, 1998)

A FRANK Lunch With Alan Eagleson

When a BBC film crew shooting a documentary about O. J. Simpson recently attempted to make lunch reservations, over half the L.A. eateries refused to allow the innocent murderer in the door. The film also showed passersby taunting and insulting Simpson as he strolled through his neighbourhood.

Alan Eagleson is not O. J. Simpson, but the former hockey czarina has suffered his share of humiliation and embarrassment ever since he was convicted of several counts of fraud and theft and sentenced to 18 months in the Big House.

With the former Great Canadian out on day parole, FRANK endeavoured to test the waters and see if Toronto's finest sports bars and drinking establishments would accept reservations for The Eagle and his entourage.

Would the maitre d's at Gretzky's, Don Cherry's, the SkyDome, etc., forgive Al's trespasses and show him the tolerance, understanding, and compassion for which Canadians are rightly famous?

Hey, business is business, right?

FRANK: I'm organizing a little coming-out luncheon for Alan Eagleson. It occurred to me that Gretzky's might be a good place to do it. Do you think you could accommodate us?

Wayne Gretzky's Restaurant: I don't see a problem with that at all. We have a couple of special requirements owing to the unique situation. Would it be possible, in terms of flatware, to have no knives or forks?

Just take away all the knives and forks?

Yes, just dull spoons.

What do you mean?

Well, it's because of the regulations of his parole.

Oh, okay.

And also, do you have a tin cup to serve beverages in?

Well, if you go on the patio, we only have plastic cups out there.

Oh, that would be good.

There's bottles, but you can just ask for pints instead if you are going to get beer. That's my best suggestion.

But, of course, the parole conditions mean we can't drink any alcohol. I assume you have some kind of security there.

We do if it is a special occasion.

There's a fellow Mr. Eagleson met in the correctional facility who will provide security, if that's okay with you.

Um, hold on a second. Let me talk to my manager. [MANAGER COMES ON]

FRANK: I was just speaking to somebody there about a dinner party for Alan Eagleson. I was unclear about the security arrangements.

We don't have security. Mike Harris has to bring his own security.

Oh, I see. Mr. Eagleson has a friend he met in the correctional facility who is going to do security.

Okay.

This fellow's name is Mommy.

Mommy?

Yes, it's his nickname. He's a big biker guy. You can't miss him.

He's going to be your security? Will he be joining you at the table?

No, he'll be keeping his eye on the door. Would there be a separate table for Mr. Eagleson's parole officer?

Yes, okay. There was something about cutlery and glassware?

Yes, it's one of these conditions of his parole.

Alan Eagleson can't have cutlery or glassware?!

No, he can have cutlery as long as it isn't knives or forks.

I'm a little confused about what his party would use.

The rest of his party would use whatever you'd normally put out, but at his setting . . .

Alan Eagleson's setting?

Yes – do you have plastic cups?

Yes, but we would normally use that only on the patio but we could do one or all . . .

Why don't you do them all so we don't embarrass Mr. Eagleson. Do you get a lot of hockey players who come in there?

Yes, when the Leafs are in town.

Carl Brewer doesn't come in there, does he? Frank Mahovolich doesn't come in?

He does come in but not frequently.

He doesn't have a reservation tonight, does he?

No.

FRANK: Would there be a table where Mr. Eagleson wouldn't have to have his back to the door? He likes to keep his eye out.

Don Cherry's Grill: There's nothing really private. People would not expect him to be there.

No?

He'd just be every day people. I mean, people are shocked when Don and Ron come up after the game.

They're not coming up tonight, are they?

I don't know. Don owns this place and he comes in whenever. He could, he could not. It all depends. I'm not sure if – I fell asleep during the hockey game last night – so I don't know if they were on. No, actually, he's in Dallas.

There wouldn't be a problem if we brought our own security, would there?

No, as long as they didn't make it evident.

It's just a couple of fellows that Mr. Eagleson met in the correctional facility.

That's fine.

Is there any kind of dress requirement? Mr. Eagleson wears an orange paper suit.

This is a joke? He wouldn't wear an orange suit. Are you talking about a jail suit?

Well…

That's only in the U.S. They're only orange in the U.S.A.

Oh, okay.

Hard Rock Cafe SkyDome: How many people are you looking at?

Well, it was originally going to be 14 or 15, but I don't think we're going to get the kind of turn out we hoped for.

Maybe as low as six. What's your security like there?

It's right inside SkyDome, so we have SkyDome security.

Could we bring Mr. Eagleson in through the kitchen?

Hmmm. Do you want to speak to my manager?

Okay.

[MANAGER COMES ON]

Do you know the way our restaurant is laid out? You want to come in through the kitchen?

Yes, he's only been on parole a short time and we want to make sure there are no difficulties.

I don't think you'd have a security problem. We don't have a lot of rough types in here.

It's mostly with other athletes we're concerned about. I guess you get a lot of athletes in there?

Yeah, but mostly during game days, so I'd say you'd be pretty safe tonight.

Okay, I notice you have memorabilia there. Do you want him to bring a photo or anything like that?

We really only collect rock 'n' roll memorabilia, but that's a nice thought. I appreciate it.

One of the conditions of his release is that there's no alcohol, so we'd prefer that nobody gets served at the table.

I don't have a problem with that, but if someone at the table asks for liquor, it's the server's job to serve.

Well, we don't want to embarrass him by it being offered.

Oh, okay.

We'd also need a separate table for his parole officer and his bodyguard.

That's fine.

Windows on SkyDome: What I can do for you is – we have corporate mini-suites that hold eight people. They're sort of semi-private, you're separated by glass partitions.

There's no metal bars on the windows, are there?

No. You're facing the field.

Okay. Do you serve beans on toast?

Well, it's an all you can eat buffet.

Mr. Eagleson really likes beans on toast.

That's kind of eccentric.

It's what he ate in, y'know, prison.

I'm sure special arrangements can be made, with enough advance notice. You just have to let us know.

Is there any way of finding out, on the night we come, who else might be there? I presume you get professional athletes there, hockey players.

On occasion we get a couple of baseball players coming through and signing autographs but it's kind of rare. More often it's the wives of players.

That's good. We didn't want any trouble. Would you like him to bring an autographed photo to put up on the wall?

I'm sure the restaurant would really appreciate that.

Have you ever had any trouble with the lights dimming in the restaurant?

No, not at all.

It's one thing he's kind of sensitive about. He tends to get worked up and start banging on the tables when the lights dim.

No, he'd be right up against the glass. That wouldn't be a problem.

FRANK: Could I also book a single table next to them for Mr. Eagleson's parole officer?

Canoe: It might not be possible to have him sitting right next to him. He can't be sitting at the same table?

Well, it's sort of a sticky situation.

Okay, well – we could seat them at the bar. It faces the kitchen, and there are good sight-lines, you can

see the west end of the city.

Okay, great, so there are good lines of sight, security-wise, we're not going to have problems. We would rather Mr. Eagleson didn't have to sit with his back to the door. Would everybody be lined up at the bar?

Well, it's normally the last place we seat people, it overlooks the kitchen.

Okay that sounds good.

So, no steak knives and a parole officer at the sushi bar. Great!

Yeah, I'd like to book a couple of tables for lunch. A table for six and a table for one.

Barberian's: Okay.

Would it be possible to have those tables next to one another?

Sure. And what's the name of the table for one?

Smith. Officer Smith.

And the table for six?

Alan Eagleson.

Ohhhhh!

Officer Smith is his parole officer.

Mr. Eagleson. Well, we have a private dining room upstairs, it's very discreet, his party of six can sit up there and Officer Smith can sit downstairs.

Well –

Or is that not possible?

No, I'm afraid he has to be there.

Well, let me just put you through to John.

John: Hello?

Yes, I was asking about a table for Alan Eagleson for tomorrow?

Yes, a table for six and a table for one. Consider it done.

(Ed. note: Barberians was where Russ Conway, Carl Brewer, Frank Mahovolich, Brad Park et al. celebrated Eagleson's conviction.)

FRANK PRANKS

(July 1, 1998)
SELLING ENERGY TO THE ARABS
Sheik Yerbouti Gets the Bomb

With opposition MPs frantic over tales of Canadian involvement in the upcoming India v. Pakistan thermonuclear jamboree, FRANK raises the stakes by offering our nuke technology to the fictitious nation of Yerbouti. Posing as a wire service reporter, we called up backbenchers to deploy this doomsday scenario of our own creation...

FRANK: We have some information about Atomic Energy Canada Ltd. negotiating a CANDU deal with a country named Yerbouti.

Art Hanger (Ref-Calgary Northeast): Yerbouti? Where's that?

It's one of the United Arab Emirates. It's an Islamic country. It looks like about a $750–million deal, but the problem is, it's one of these no-money-down deals. If the oil prices stay low, and the Yerboutis decide they don't feel like paying ...

Hanger

How are we going to collect? We could always take it out of their hide in oil.

I guess. But oil's not worth much. In the light of the Pakistan-India situation, there are some questions about the stability of this place.

Absolutely. It's right on the doorstep of Sadaam Hussein territory.

Exactly. And apparently they have a relationship with Pakistan already, which as you know has a well-developed nuclear weapons capability.

It floors me, first of all, why Canada would stick their neck out to this degree to sell this kind of technology and equipment to a country that is in that location. It's a well-known fact that Iraq has always had their eye on that region. They've been into that spot before.

On the map, it looks like a fairly strategic location. It's right on the Strait of Baba Ganouj, which connects to the Persian Gulf of Onan.

Yeah, I would think that our American friends would not be happy knowing that Canada is involved in this kind of arrangement. I really don't see how they can be silent about it, and if they don't know, they should be informed.

The other factor here is Yerbouti's long-standing conflict with Yemen and South Yemen. If one of the nations were to develop nuclear capability, it would destabilize the whole Red Sea area.

My goodness, yes. I don't think it's an acceptable arrangement at all. I'm surprised our government is letting it go ahead or even supporting the arrangement. I don't see that as a valuable activity to be involved.

Apparently, Sergio Marchi's riding has the highest percentage of Yerbouti-Canadians in the country.

Oh, really? And he apparently has had contact with Sheik Ashtar Yerbouti who is the strongman of the country. So, there's questions about Marchi's connections to Sheik Yerbouti.

I don't know if Marchi has ever been wise when it comes to supporting policy that is detrimental to the country or that region. I don't think our allies would be very pleased with him if that is the connection.

How familiar are you with Yerbouti itself?

The United Arab Emirates – you know, I've met some of their councillors. I've talked to some of them, but apart from that I don't know a lot about the country.

Have you met Sheik Yerbouti?

No, I haven't.

Do you have any Yerbouti-Canadians in your riding?

I may have. It's interesting to note – no, I don't think I do. No, I shouldn't say that, because I do have a lot of Arabic people in my area.

It's an Islamic nation. So you've got to address the issue of terrorism.

Well, the Islamic side of the equation cannot be ignored. Not to say that everybody of Islamic faith can be lumped into that category, but that is a fact of life one can't ignore.

Peter Stoffer (NDP Sackville-Eastern Shore): Jerbouti?
FRANK: No, Yerbouti.

Jerbouti, I think it is. With a "J."

No, it's with a "Y."

Okay. *That's* a good place to sell CANDU reactors. Perfect. What a bunch of idiots. What a bunch of idiots. It's an Islamic republic. It doesn't sound like the most stable place, but its location is strategically important. There's talk of possible weapons testing in the desert. They've aligned themselves with

Cadman

Pakistan and there are fears they're going to detonate a test.

That's what the world needs. I wouldn't be too surprised. It would be most unfortunate. The government is continuing to supply the world with nuclear technology. If it was up to me, I'd shut down the entire nuclear sale program in a heartbeat. We're literally giving away this technology.

In this case, there was no money down. **Oh, we finally sold to a country that may have some cash in their hands. Are we that desperate for cash? Are we actually going to put uranium or plutonium in those reactors sitting there in a hot spot? And we know very well that we don't test what goes on afterwards. We sell them, and we walk away.**

Yeah.

It's like your car dealer when he sells you a car. He doesn't test how fast you drive. He doesn't see if you're drinking and driving. He just sells you a car and gets out of it.

Right. Right.

What really pissed me off, prior to me entering politics, was Sergio Marchi when he was environment minister, actually changing the regulations in order to sell CANDU reactors to China.

Interesting that you say that. I've got a StatsCan report that says Marchi's riding has the highest concentration of Yerbouti-Canadians in the country.

What a coincidence. I can assure you I am totally against selling nuclear reactors to anybody.

FRANK: We have reports of AECL negotiating a CANDU deal with a country called Yerbouti in the Middle East. It's a $750-million reactor deal.

Chuck Cadman (Ref-Surrey North): Well that's the first I heard of it. I have
no idea of what that country's track record is. I've heard the name, but that's it.

There are fears that it would destabilize the region. Yerbouti is not above rekindling hostilities with South Yemen. There's been a historical conflict dating back to 89 A.D.

It's a powder keg. Again, I wouldn't want to make any hard and fast comment, but if there's even the slightest possibility we're going to supply somebody with the technology to manufacture nuclear arms, then I'm almost dead set against it. We better make sure we know what we're doing here.

On first blush, this place looks like it's quite wealthy from oil revenues. It looks like we've given them the reactors with no money down, so Canadian taxpayers are on the hook.

The only comment is that we better be doing our homework. We've got our fingerprints all over India and Pakistan. Let's not go for more.

Borotsik

FRANK: We're getting reports that Atomic Energy of Canada may have been involved with an Islamic country in the Middle-East called Yerbouti. There's fear that a nuclear Yerbouti could destabilize the whole region.

Rick Borotsik (PC-Brandon Souris): I figure that the whole Persian Gulf area is pretty much destabilized right now. CANDU reactors obviously have – they produce pluto-
nium. Plutonium is used in the manufacture of nuclear devices. If this government doesn't think that plutonium [in India] didn't come from CANDU reactors, they're sadly mistaken or lying to themselves. We are part of the problem. Yerbouti I never heard of.

They export oil to Pakistan. They now have weapons grade plutonium from the reactors and the Pakistanis may be lending some of their nuclear technology in exchange for oil. There may also be some weapons testing in the desert. This is an area of concern.

Very much so. It's an area of a great deal of concern. Obviously, it's very disconcerting.

Apparently Yerbouti has had a long history of conflict with Yemen and South Yemen. They've been at peace for only 36 years, so it's a tense situation.

Okay. And there's a $750-million loan requirement to develop a nuclear technology. So they've got a reactor and they've got the technology coming from Pakistan, they can mix it all up.

Rick Casson (Ref-Lethbridge): If it is indeed taking place, we hope it would not be handled similarly to the China and Turkey deals, where environment assessments are bypassed and we have to borrow [sic] these people the money to buy these things. It's a vicious circle. I think the concern is more in terms of the security and stability. **I think Canada has to sit back and look at the customers they'll accept for these things because of what is happening in India and Pakistan. There's no doubt the technology they learned from us is fueling the issue.**

There's also the element of terrorism. Their leader, Sheik Ashtar Yerbouti doesn't have the best reputation internationally.

I'm going to have to do some background on this. What's the name of the country?

Yerbouti. Yerbouti. Y-E-R-B-O-U-T-I.

And where is it?

It's on the Gulf of Onan. You know where that is?

Yep.

It's near Baba Ganouj.

I'm going to have to poke around a bit and see what's up.

Apparently, Sergio Marchi has the highest concentration of Yerbouti-Canadians in his riding, and they are really involved in his riding association.

Is that right? That's very interesting.

John Reynolds (Ref-West Vancouver-Sunshine Coast): The government makes these deals with these countries, but do they have the ability to pay for them? And do they have the security?

FRANK: That's just it. It seems like it's not a very stable nation. They have a long history of conflict with their neighbours in Onan. There's also rekindled hostilities with South Yemen. If one of these nations has nuclear weapons...

It's not even that. It's an unstable nation and you've got a plant with nuclear capability and they come in and bomb it or something – if it's not secure in its own right – the plant itself could become a Chernobyl in the wrong hands.

Right. Right.

What really ticks me off – I hear these stories, horror stories to some degree, because of the way we take this money, which is Canadian taxpayers' money, and give it to people who already have lots of money. And yet, in my own constituency this week, we have employees trying to buy back a hotel that's in receivership and the government won't help them at all. It just bothers me. Where are our priorities?

In this case, there are fears they're going to conduct some weapons tests in the Yerbouti desert. There's only a few nomads and camels there but . . .

What if one of them goes off, if we had a nuclear plant there, and one of those things were to stray off or a terrorist were to get in. You don't put them in places where there is not stability.

That's the other question – terrorism. It is an Islamic country.

Yup.

Do you know anything about Yerbouti itself?

Very little. I know where it is and I know that part of the world, and that's what scares me.

Do you know this Sheik Yerbouti guy? He's the guy who negotiated the deal with AECL.

No. I'd like to know what guarantees they have.

(After a few more hours of this foolishness, Hugh Blakeney, press secretary to NDP leader Alexa McDoughnut and

Reynolds

Alexa

son of former Saskatchewan premier Allan Blakeney, calls to find out what's going on . . .)

FRANK: It's quite a wealthy nation and there is some suggestion that AECL has sold a $750-million reactor to Yerbouti. It's one of these no-money-down deals.

Hugh Blakeney: Normally, we say we sell our reactors for the purpose of generating hydro electrical or energy. The United Arab Emirates is not short of enegy as far as I know.

Well, that would raise some interesting questions, wouldn't it?

Yeah. If they're not short of energy, what are they short of? Nuclear technology?

That would seem to be the case. It's a very wealthy nation.

And I'm not incorrect – they have access to considerable oil reserves?

Yes, they do. It's not a very stable country. It has two traditional enemies – Catarrh to the north and Onan to south. This conflict goes back to something like 89 A.D. There's been conflict with Yemen and South Yemen in the past.

Right.

If the Yerbouti oil dollars align themselves with Pakistan, it may embolden Pakistan and cause them to become more aggressive to India. It's the domino effect.

Well, obviously I don't know much about it. I can't comment. It's an eye-opener.

FRANK PRANKS

(July 29, 1998)

Gillian Guess in Pre-Production

Throughout her trial on obstruction of justice charges, disgraced jurist Gillian Guess fantasized aloud about selling her life story for a book or movie deal. Guess hoped to cash in on the tale of the passionate love affair she conducted with Peter Gill while she sat on the jury that found him innocent of murder.

Since her conviction, however, little has been heard about rendering Guess's story for the silver screen. But, Son of Sam legislation notwithstanding, FRANK has learned that Gillian Guess: The Movie is still very much on the rails, even if Gillian herself is en route to the Big House.

Posing as an aide to imaginary film producer "Marty Green," FRANK called up Guess's Vancouver-based "entertainment lawyer," Andrew Atkins, to talk turkey . . .

FRANK: I'm trying to reach Gillian Guess. I understand you represent her. Is she contracted with anyone right now?

She is not contracted with anyone. There has been quite a bit of interest, primarily from Canadian-affiliated companies out of the States. That's pretty much where it sits at this moment. Nothing definitive has been done but there's two or three offers that have been bandied about.

I guess we're getting in late on the game.

Well, I'm not sure you're getting in late. As I have told everyone all along, if there is interest from multiple parties, we're not going to conclude any deals until we've given all the parties an opportunity to consider what the offer is. To be quite blunt, that's how I plan to maximize my client's interest.

Right, of course. Who have you had interest from, so far?

We've had interest from Alliance-Atlantis, Columbia, an independent producer out of L.A., and an independent producer out of Toronto.

Has anybody pitched a story idea?

The story, I think, is fairly self-evident. Basically, what they're trying to do is get Gillian's and her family's story rights, then proceed from there.

Right.

The offers are in the – I'll give you some ballpark figures – the offers are generally around $10,000 U.S. up front, $25,000 on set up, which would be on the network buy, and then between $100,000 and $125,000 on the back end.

Yeah, okay. That's approximately what we were thinking.

They're not outrageous numbers, but they're significant from Canadian terms, for sure.

It's not just a Canadian story obviously.

Well, no. One guy phoned up and said, "Jeez, with the conviction, that's it. We're out of the game." In some respects, that creates the story.

I agree.

If you're on the Gillian Guess side of the equation, if you believe the way this law is being characterized and used is not appropriate, then a conviction makes it that much more powerful. It really indicates how far things can come awry.

Yeah. All I've seen is the media cover-age of it.

I've seen guys who are pretty decent journalists, generally speaking, referring to her – this is a direct quote – "matronly hips."

That's pretty cruel.

Exactly. Really, these guys, seasoned professionals, have been reduced to turning this into a tabloid issue. Regardless of what side of the legal issue you fall, it's an extraordinarily important legal issue that's been undertaken here, yet the press has been reduced to talking about her "matronly hips."

She is an actor herself?

I think she's done some stand-in stuff and some bit part stuff.

Would she see an involvement with this project if it were to proceed?

I don't believe so. Unless you did it as a documentary.

No, no.

You would have to fictionalize portions of it. You'd have to dramatize it. To that extent, I don't think you'd find you have a professional actress. You'd find that you have a person who is just like you and I.

Marty has been bouncing around ideas – he's got a good relationship with Mickey Rourke – he's talking of him as the Peter Gill character.

Mickey Rourke would be a very suitable character for that. That's an interesting spin. I have seen stuff with Mickey Rourke – he's a great actor, but sometimes he goes off the edge.

Have any of your people been talking to HBO?

No. That would be a logical place . . .

Marty has done a number of HBO things in the past. He did *Song of Silence* with Mickey Rooney and a Carole Burnette thing, *Tender as the Night is Long* . . . . Whether a Canadian story would carry a network deal – maybe, maybe not.

Given the numbers that have been

bandied about, it would have to carry some kind of U.S. sale.

Right. Who are you negotiating that with?

There's been a number of people: *Dateline, Hard Copy*, basically the tabloid-esque.

What kind of numbers are you talking about there?

Quite frankly, we haven't talked any numbers. We just talked. Are you a lawyer?

No, I just work with Marty. I'm here in Ottawa. We're actually talking with Sheldon Kennedy's people this week.

Oh, really. There's an interesting

song – I work with Barney Bentall. Barney did a song called, Oh, Shelley, he did some time ago.

Oh, really?

Barney and Shelley are friends. Interesting to keep that in mind.

Okay, I'll be in touch.

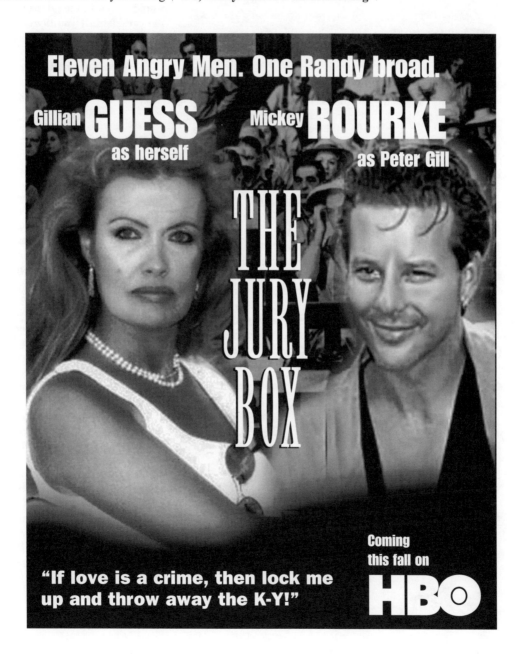

Eleven Angry Men. One Randy broad.

Gillian **GUESS**
as herself

Mickey **ROURKE**
as Peter Gill

THE JURY BOX

Coming
this fall on
HBO

"If love is a crime, then lock me up and throw away the K-Y!"

FRANK PRANKS

(September 9, 1998)
The Copps-Clinton Connection

Desperate for a domestic angle on the Oral Office oval sex crisis, FRANK conjured a ludicrous rumour linking Heritage Minister Sheila Copps with President Bill Clinton. We posed as wire service reporter "Nelson Eddy" of United Press Services' bureau in Ottawa and called up a gaggle of Reform MPs for comment.

Now entering the studio are today's contestants . . .

FRANK: We have leaked reports out of the Clinton grand jury about a Canadian politician named Copps.

Randy White (Ref-Langley-Abbotsford): Oh God.

Ken Starr asked Clinton some pretty pointed questions about a weekend in June 1996 [that Clinton] spent with [Copps] at Chesapeake Bay near Washington.

No kidding? Hooo, hoo, hooo. That doesn't surprise me.

What would your reaction be?

My immediate reaction is: it's about time some of the other side of the Liberals started to surface. What definitely doesn't surprise me is that name. They're outstanding at hiding these issues and we know they exist, but the Canadian media doesn't seem to like digging them up.

What do you mean? Personal things?

Yes. We get anything at all on us [Reform]. You don't have to look very far with the Liberals, but we don't care to start on that avenue. It's about time the media started looking at some of the actors on the other side.

What do you think she should do?

White: Well, if that is in fact true, nobody is as good as digging that sort of stuff up as the Americans. You know, I think the Prime Minister has some decisions to make on morality and integrity. Let's see how he will protect this one. Thus far, he hasn't taken any action against any of his ministers for anything.

Do you think we should be considering resignation on this?

White: I think she should be given a chance to confirm or deny. And she would be put in the same position as the president. If you deny, and it is confirmed, then definitely. What a position to be in.

Apparently, the FBI has some physical evidence.

This isn't FRANK Magazine?

No. United Press Services.

This hasn't come out yet?

They're not going to move it on the wire until 3:45 pm.

Okay.

Jay Hill (Ref-Prince George-Peace River): I'm amazed with the preoccupation of North American media — and I include the Canadian media — with the White House soap opera. I would think for us, there is enough for Canadians to focus on, with our loonie and slumping economy, rather than a foreign country's president's infidelity.

FRANK: Mr. Starr was asking about an inscribed book of Dilbert cartoons that [Clinton] had given [Copps].

There again, the only person who should be concerned about this is — I'm sorry, I don't remember his name — is Sheila's husband.

Austin.

Austin. He is the one who should be concerned about that. Not you and I. If there was a breach of trust there. To me it's very reminiscent of the events — the unfortunate events — surrounding Princess Diana. I guess in that case, some of the investigation you can argue is

appropriate. Poor Diana, she was just hounded by the media over in Europe.

Do you think that will happen to Mrs. Copps?

I hope not. I don't see any point to it. What would be the argument from the public's point of view? That she somehow revealed state secrets?

Grant Hill (Ref-Macleod): Who knows? These kinds of rumours are easy to start. He does not have a good reputation in terms of his personal character when it comes to women. It's a shame that someone of his stature doesn't have the control to look after what is a pretty important part of life.

FRANK: But if this is coming out in the grand jury testimony . . .

Yeah, but good luck to them. That doesn't sound like much of a hook to hang your hat on.

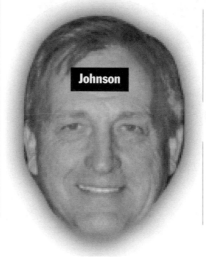

Hill

Apparently Starr was asking about a joke in the White House about "calling the Copps." It was some kind of euphemism.

Well, to my knowledge — and these kind of rumours are circulated about attractive politicians — I've never heard anything about Sheila Copps that would suggest she is immoral at all.

Do you think this may affect her ability to function in cabinet?

Only if there is some substance to it. I mean, Clinton has besmirched the office of the president. The headline in the local paper here was "Liar, Liar."

It would be a shame to see it besmirch the Canadian cabinet, too.

It would. But there would have to be some pretty strong evidence.

Dale Johnson (Ref-Wetaskiwin): I don't want to comment on that. This is typical American politics. Let's slag the hell out of whoever is in power. The Watergate break-ins and all the rest of it, it's politics at its worse.

FRANK: Do you think it's appropriate that Ms. Copps would be dragged into this?

I don't know. I guess the grand jury can ask whatever questions they feel are relevant. I don't know what rationale they would use in terms of relevance here.

What about the propriety of a woman in cabinet, who is married, having a relationship with an American politician?

I don't think that's proper. The same way I don't think extramarital affairs are proper no matter who you are or what you do.

Do you think it's grounds for resignation?

Johnson

Don't want to get into that. It's just too much speculation.

FRANK: Apparently Sheila Copps' name came up in the testimony.

Inky Mark (Ref-Dauphin-Swan River): Sheila Copps' name came up?

Yes.

In the testimony?

What about her ability to function effectively in cabinet if there is a media feeding frenzy?

I think we have to delay judgement. If it's private business. It's nobody's business how I spend my weekends when I'm away from the House. If it isn't a breach of rules, her job as a minister, then it's nobody's business. But you can't be guilty by association. Her intent was maybe just a social visit. I don't know. I will resign my judgement until I hear further details.

FRANK: There were questions Starr was asking about a weekend they spent together in June 1996.

Gary Lunn (Ref-Saanich-Gulf Islands): You've caught me totally off guard. I don't have all the details. I haven't spoken with Ms. Copps. I'm so wrapped up in so many other issues. You've thrown a curve at me.

The consensus seems to be that she should make some kind of statement to clarify.

I wouldn't even go that far until we have more information. Did you say it was confirmed it was Sheila Copps?

Inky

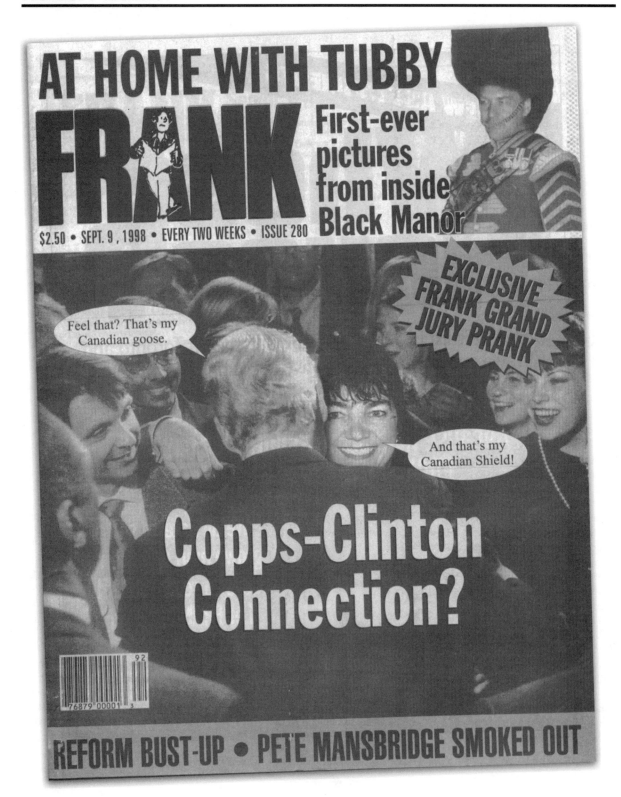

Yes, they originally reported it as Shirley but later amended it to Sheila.

And that's the same Sheila Copps that's sitting in the House of Commons?

Yes.

From what you've told me, I'm sure it will hit the airways and Ms. Copps will make a statement. There are not allegations of wrong doing there.

She doesn't seem like the kind of woman he would be interested in.

I'm not going to analyze the kind of women Mr. Clinton is interested in. I'm not even going to go down that road.

One point that was raised was whether she could function in cabinet if she was being hounded the same way Lewinsky was hounded.

Let's put it this way. If it comes out that there was a weekend with the president of the United States, yeah, I would agree that the prime minister would have some tough decisions to make.

 Lee Morrison (Ref-Cypress Hills-Grasslands):

Is this a hoax?

FRANK: No. I couldn't believe it when I heard it myself. Apparently there was a weekend they spent together.

I'm not going to touch that one with a ten foot pole. I'm sorry. You're sure you're not with FRANK Magazine?

Is that a political magazine?

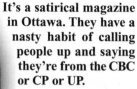

It's a satirical magazine in Ottawa. They have a nasty habit of calling people up and saying they're from the CBC or CP or UP.

Oh really? I wasn't aware of that. I just moved here.

It's sort of a *Mad Magazine* for grown-ups.

Oh, okay.

This is on that level?

Yes, apparently there was testimony from someone who worked in the White House that there was a euphemism they used among staff about "calling the Copps."

You got my immediate reaction. I don't know, I'd rather stay away from that one. I'll certainly be yukking it up with my associates.

Do you think it might make it difficult for her to function as a cabinet minister?

I don't know. She got away with something much more severe than this when she did her little ploy of "If they don't scrap the GST, I'll resign." I took an extraordinarily dim view of that, yet she came up smelling like a rose.

But this sort of thing would go to the character issue, wouldn't it?

Didn't the other? She made a bold statement that if "A" didn't

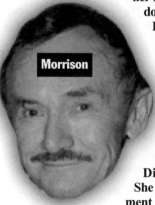

happen she would quit.

Do you think she would have the same kind of wiggle room on something like this?

I don't know. The whole thing is so bizarre.

She doesn't seem like the kind of woman Clinton would be attracted to.

Morrison: I know I wouldn't be — hey, that's off the record.

 Deepak Obhrai (Ref-Calgary East): You just blew me out of the water, my friend.

FRANK: There was a weekend in 1996 when Copps and Clinton were both staying at family friend's house not that far from Washington.

And?

And Starr pointedly asked him about the nature of his relationship and Clinton refused to discuss it. Obviously, something is happening here.

I think it is inappropriate for me to comment on something that is just a rumour.

Well, the leak has been substantiated. Some of the other opposition members I've spoken to are calling for some kind of statement from Copps. The media attention might make it difficult for her to function in cabinet.

If there is any uncertainty, Ms. Copps should clear the air. I don't call for her resignation. If she has anything to say, she should say it.

It seems to me this is a family values issue. What do you think of someone holding a cabinet post who may have been having an affair with the president?

I think until this thing is a proven fact, that there was a substantial

relationship, then we can comment on it. If there are any doubts created, Ms. Copps has to clarify the doubts.

There is a report from Washington that the FBI is trying to get a hold of some clothing Copps had — some kind of Bay pant suit.

Well, these are all speculation.

Our Washington bureau has confirmed that the FBI does have in their possession a tan pant suit that was owned by Ms. Copps. I don't know what they're doing with it.

Would all these things not lead to rumours? All we ask for is Ms. Copps to clarify the situation. You really blew me this time, buddy. You really blew me.

Have you ever met Clinton?

No.

I'm just wondering if she's the kind of woman he would be interested in.

Oh, no. I've never met Clinton. I'm a first-term MP.

Do you think she's attractive?

No comment. I don't know these people on a personal level.

 FRANK: I'm trying to get some response from Opposition MPs about Ms. Copps being involved in this high profile case.

Myron Thompson (Ref-Wild Rose) Phew. I don't really have anything to say. I just don't believe it.

How do you feel about a Canadian cabinet minister in this position?

I guess we should wait and see what comes of it. If there's any truth in it, she should probably make a statement. I can't believe somebody's conscience. I find it hard to believe.

There will be enormous media interest in her now.

I'll be watching. It is awfully difficult to determine the future. What would be in store for anyone in that predicament. It's certainly a wait-and-see thing for me.

If you have someone who is minister of heritage, in a leadership role — how appropriate is it? Ms. Copps is a married woman.

Based on the knowledge I do know, what has been reported in regards to Clinton. I think it's disgraceful. That's about all I have to say. I certainly don't condone any activities of that nature.

Maybe she should temporarily resign to clear it up.

I hadn't heard a thing about it. I'll be watching. I don't know what the truth is. Gotta know the facts. I've been watching the news pretty regular, but I haven't seen it.

(December 2, 1998)

Polishing a Turd

With his recent ascension to Companion of the Order of Canada, we at FRANK realize we have been dreadfully mistaken about Byron Muldoon all these years. To do our part to assist in his rehabilitation, FRANK phoned various worthy organizations to offer the services of our Greatest Living Irishman. Posing as a representative with Devon and Associates, a public relations firm in Ottawa, we offered to "reposition" Mr. Muldoon for the next millennium.

FRANK: Mr. Mulroney has expressed a profound interest in working with you.
Sally Errey: With Earthsave?
Yes, perhaps doing some public service work . . . remaking his image, like Princess Diana, but he doesn't want to do anything dangerous.

That's good, because we're a non-political group which is why people haven't heard of us, because we don't chain ourselves to cows or anything. Our main mission is to educate people . . . to adopt a healthier diet.
That's good. He's been trying to cut down on his meat intake, but he has a weakness for emu meat.
All right.
What kind of role can you see Mr. Mulroney playing?
I'm not sure, maybe he'd like to come and speak to us. We have monthly potlucks where we often invite speakers. Would he be able to bring some emu?
[LAUGHS]. **I guess so, but most of our members are vegetarians.**

Bruce Webster (Alberta Sugar Beet Association.)
FRANK: Mr. Mulroney feels his prime ministership, as with the beet, was a fairly maligned vegetable. I'm calling to gauge your interest in working together for mutual benefit.
Sure. We're gearing up for the World Agriculture talks next year and there's a great deal of potential.
Yes, it has been an ongoing concern of Mr. Mulroney's that history will prove the beet a very tasty vegetable. He is very interested in reaching out to you to ensure, that as a vegetable, it doesn't get relegated to the compost heap like his prime ministership did.
Um-hum.
You don't promote any Swiss

varieties of [beets] do you?
No. No.
Good, cause he's a little concerned about being involved with anything to do with Switzerland.
I'm a subscriber to *Saturday Night* so I've read all about it.
What did you read?
The excerpts from the book, that the whole thing to do with Airbus was a travesty, and pursued quite viciously by the federal government on an unjustified basis.
Good. I just want to clarify one last thing. You don't have any association with Stevie Cameron then, do you?
No. No, I don't.
That's good to know.
I supported him in the leadership campaign against Joe Clark.

Stephen Pope (President Solar Energy Society.)
FRANK: We're involved in repositioning his image for the new millennium.
Jesus Christ! Well, Joe Clark's back, so I suppose we can't wait another 20 years for Here-Comes-Brian.
Yes, well, he expressed a profound interest in doing some kind of promotional work.
You're kidding!
I think I should tell you Mr. Mulroney is not looking for any kind of remuneration for this. He has expressed an interest in perhaps getting a solar panel set up in his back garden sometime, but he doesn't want any pay.
Yes, I can understand the benefits that would accrue through this sort of involvement.

Margaret Pounder (President, American Emu Association, Idaho.)
FRANK: Is there some kind of role that you could imagine him playing?
What does he know about emus?
The emu is Mr. Mulroney's favourite fowl and as Prime Minister served it

often to foreign dignitaries in his office. He feels that the emu has received a bit of a bad rap, a little like himself while he was in office.

Birds of a feather type of thing?

Yes. He figures he could identify well with the emu.

I like this.

He was wondering if whether there was some kind of mutually beneficial arrangement that we could come to?

Well, let me ponder this a bit.

This is something we haven't been approached on in the last few years. We have some real strong

constituents in the Canadian market that I'm sure he could be very helpful to.

Yes, he has a lot of friends in the poultry industry.

Rev. Glenn Penner (Development Director, Voice of the Martyrs Inc., Mississauga.)

FRANK: He feels that he has gone through a period of unwanted persecution, and he wants to help those in similar straits.

That's interesting.

Aah, baa,

baa, this is something I just wasn't expecting. I voted for the guy. I just moved from Alberta, so I did vote for the guy.

Tell me, I don't know much about your organization.

We uphold religious liberty for all groups, but in our case we are focusing particularly on the persecution of Christians worldwide. We don't [BURBLE, BURBLE] within the historical sense of what Christianity is.

Is there any program to help people like Mr. Mulroney who were crucified by the liberal press?

Not particularly. Most of what we do is overseas, so for us to tie together anything here in Canada with that . . . I'm not going to say it, forget it. One of the friends of our ministry, our work, he puts it this way. He says, listen, when they start dragging kids into slavery in B.C., then I'll say we have real persecution in Canada.

Do you have any hesitation about working with Mr. Mulroney?

The fact of the matter, I'll be honest, I'd be kind of uncomfortable tying the way he has been treated with the persecution of Christians in other countries.

Why is that?

. . . oh boy . . .

I think if we're going to have a relationship we should be honest with each other.

I think it will diminish the fact of what these people are actually having to go through in these parts of the world, where they lose their homes, their children get sold into slavery, they're thrown into prison without any possibility of fair trial . . .

I guess Mr. Mulroney coming from Westmount, would . . .

. . . look a little bit weird. He still has his wealth. Yes, he's been mistreated and all that,

FRANK

Left Coast
Loonies Log On
cyberRachel

POLISHING
A TURD
THE RESURRECTION
OF
BYRON
MULDOON

Paper War: Globe Clobbers Tubby

Michele Landsberg: Starshine Girl

$2.50 • NOV. 19, 1998 • EVERY TWO WEEKS • ISSUE 285

FRANK PRANKS

and misunderstood from a political perspective, and from the media, certainly. But I am very careful not to put him in the same camp. In both cases it's suffering, but to put it together, it would be a little bit of a stretch.

Cocaine Anonymous, Toronto.

FRANK: Mr. Mulroney has always liked Eric Clapton's song, and he wants to help people with cocaine addiction.

Wow, okay!

Mr. Mulroney has had several close friends who have had problems with alcohol. I guess Cocaine Anon would run pretty much on the same basis as AA, would it?

[kids in background]
[WHISPERING]:
We replace that "A" word with the "C" word, and all other mind-altering drugs, cause when we first started it some people thought cannabis wasn't a chemical, so we had to include all mind altering.

Would Nyquil be included as mind altering?

That depends. Nyquil does include alcohol, you know.

What kind of role can you imagine Mr. Mulroney playing? Could you see him in some kind of public relations role?

No. Our public relations is based on attraction rather than promotion.

Right, cause he knows a lot of people on Bay Street, Wall Street, moves in those circles, where a lot of people sometimes need a little something to take off the edge.

You know . . . Eric Clapton is very popular and he's building a facility down in Antigua.

Would you be interested in organizing some sort of golf tournament in Mr.

Mulroney's name? Brian loves the beach.

Susan Caron-Richer (Esperanto Association, Ottawa.)

FRANK: Mr. Mulroney feels bilingualism has failed and that Canada needs a third way. He usually charges a $45,000 speaking fee, but he is willing to waive that to raise awareness on issues of concern to the Esperanto community.

What is it he'd do?

I'm sure he could bring a lot to your community, perhaps by doing some public service announcements?

Em-hmm, sure, okay, yeah. Esperanto could use any type of help, I suppose.

By any chance, do you have any other world leaders promoting Esperanto, because Mr. Mulroney is very concerned about who he might be associated with.

Not that I know of.

How do you say Baby Doc Duvalier in Esperanto?

That's a name, so that doesn't really change it. You can change it, but a lot of people feel that a name's a name and it's not required to change it.

Minister Benjamin Mohammed (Nation of Islam, New York.)

FRANK: Mr. Mulroney has seen *Do the Right Thing* several times, and in private life, he feels it's the right time to lend himself and his name to helping race relations in North America.

Yes. If he could drop me a line, expressing his intentions, I would write back, expressing our intentions, and I think we could begin a dialogical relationship that may lead to us doing something together.

Right. Mr. Mulroney, as with Mr. Farrakhan, believes he has been unfairly represented in the mainstream...

Yeah, you can write me at the Mohammed Mosque, Number 7, 106-08 West 127 St, New York, New York, 10027.

As you might know, Mr. Mulroney is of Irish extraction, and as the Irish are known as the niggers of Europe . . .

Yes, sir.

. . . that Mr. Mulroney feels that he can identify quite well with the plight of black Americans . . .

Yes, sir . . . the whole issue of living in the world where the affirmation of the oneness of humanity, needs to be done. You see, racism is the problem, but racism is not the solution. So you transcend the racial problem with the oneness of humanity. Of course, in Islam, we affirm the oneness of God.

Right. Now would Mr. Mulroney have to convert to Islam if he was going to work with you?

No, not at all.

(January 12, 1999)

What's in the Cards for '99?

Who wouldn't like to know what the new year holds? Besides Dalton McGuinty. And who could be more adept at prognostication, more attuned to the music of the spheres than the witchy men and women employed by America's leading psychic help-lines.

On behalf of public figures with less time on their hands than satirists, FRANK called a number of spirit guides to ask the question burning in the fetid bosoms of Mel, Garth, Evan et al. To whit, what does 1999 hold? Read the following and find out, for only $3.99 a minute, U.S.

Mel Lastman

Xavier: What can I do for you, Mel?

FRANK: I gotta know, is Ginger ever going to rejoin the Spice Girls? This thing's been driving me nuts.

You want to know if Ginger is going to rejoin the Spice Girls?

Yeah. Nobody's like Ginger. Noooobody!

Didn't she leave to go solo?

Yeah, what do you see in the cards for her?

The cards definitely see a good future for her.

Okay then. Tell me something else. Is my wife going to get kidnapped again?

You want to know whether your wife is going to get kidnapped, again?

Yeah.

Why? Do you want your wife to get kidnapped again?

Er, no. It's just, some days she drives me a little around the bend.

Why would she get kidnapped?

I'm mayor of a world class city. I got a square named after me. It's great.

Your wife got kidnapped before?

Oh, sure. A few years back.

Ah, what'd they do? Hold her for ransom?

Yeah, I guess so. To be honest, I didn't

pay much attention at the time. It's a megacity.

Well Mel, I feel that was a one-off situation. I don't see it happening again.

Could you deal again? Just, you know, to be on the safe side?

Andy Scott

FRANK: Will I ever get over my fear of flying? I had a bad experience once and it cost me my job.

Grace: Ohh. Cause you're afraid of flying?

No. Some prick overheard me talking

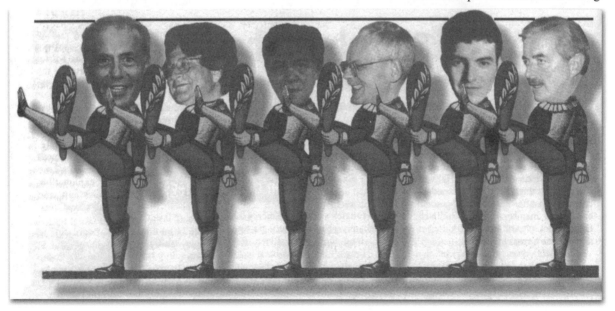

FRANK PRANKS

about Hughie.

Who's Hughie?

I'd rather not talk about it.

Oh, okay. And he did something to you?

No, but the media got hold of it and things just snowballed.

Did you work for the airlines?

No.

You were just a passenger? Oh, my goodness! But now you want to fly again?

Yes.

Well, my nephew, what he did was he learned how to fly. Once he got a grip he became an excellent pilot. Now he wants to fly commercial.

Well, that would kill two birds with one stone. And I could talk all I want about Hughie.

My advice, Andy, is forget all about Hughie.

Mark Tewksbury

FRANK: Hello, my name is Mark, and I just wanted to tell you I'm gay, I'm a screaming queen.

Bonnie: Oh…[SEVERAL SECOND PAUSE AT $3.99]. Do you have a question for me, Mark?

No, I just wanted to tell you in case your psychic line ever wants to use me for promotional work. I'm a former Olympian, you know, and I thought it would be best to be up-front about my sexuality now so it doesn't cause any problems later on.

Uh, okay?

Stanley Faulder

FRANK: How much longer do I have to live?

Candy: When were you born Stanley?

May 5, 1939.

Nineteen thirty what?

Can we make this snappy? The screws are waiting to take me back to my cell.

The what?

I'm on Death Row. Don't have much time.

You're on Death Row and you what?

Listen: I got the guards waiting to take me back to my cell. Do you want to step on it?

Really? How long have you been on Death Row?

About thirty years.

Thirty years? Oh wow. It looks like you have another twenty years to live. Really?

Unless you're on your way there now?

Lady, I'm already on Death Row.

I know that. So why you calling those guys scrooges? What are you on Death Row for?

Murder, I murdered someone.

Only one and you're on Death Row? This is Texas.

Oh, my God. You're gonna get the needle.

Garth Drabinsky

Linda: What's your last name, Garth?

FRANK: Drabinsky.

Oh, I thought you were going to say Brooks. What's your date of birth?

October 27, 1948.

What city are you calling from?

Toronto

Okay, have you talked to a psychic before?

No. My company has gone into receivership and I feel like such a loser.

Okay, let's get through it. I'm going to be shuffling your cards. I want you to tell me when to stop.

[WAITS THREE SECONDS AT $3.99 A MINUTE] Stop!

Okay, ordinarily this card doesn't come up first, but are you going through some legal litigation or have to sign some kind of contracts?

Bingo.

This card represents balance, avoid extremes. Try to be fair. This is a card of justice and it's obviously leading to legal matters. Whatever contracts you're signing or getting involved in, make sure you go through it thoroughly.

Do the cards say anything about what line of work I should get into now?

Hang on; I'm just trying to get you through this part real quick. Be real careful about how you sign things and it will turn out to your benefit. If you don't and you miss something then it's not going to turn out well. I do have here that you're going on a fresh start.

I was wondering if you think I should start my own psychic friends network?

Um. . . . It's telling me that as long as you're guided by your inner self, rather than logic . . . you know that small voice that talks to you, that knows your innermost thoughts?

Myron?

Ah, listen to that, cause that's kind of like your soul and it's been around for ever and ever . . .

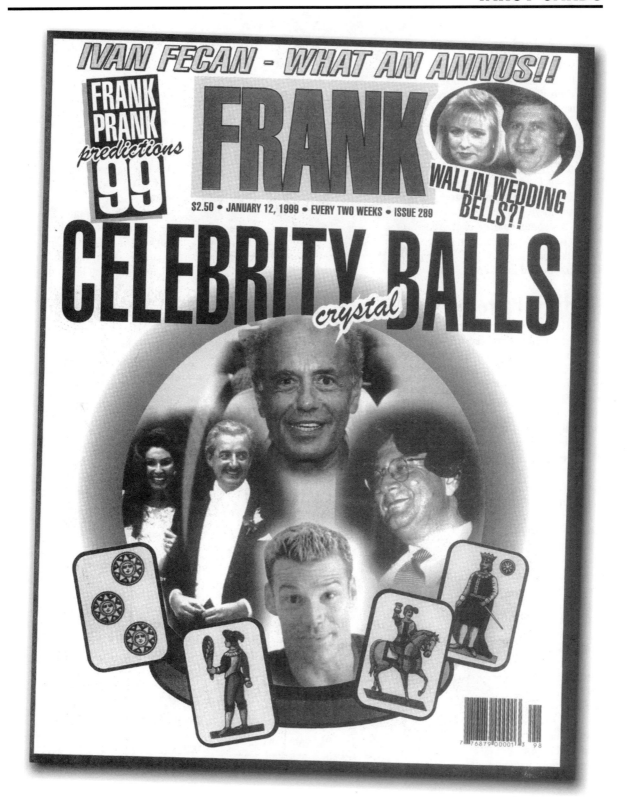

FRANK PRANKS

It's also a bit, you know, psychic too, maybe?

Um, so it kind of knows. If it tells you that's what you should be into, then do it. You weren't real positive about decisions you've made in the past. Hooking up with this guy – I wish you had talked to me before! – is the whole reason why you've been this low and haven't been able to move on and obtain more money faster.

I was wondering if I called back we could cut some kind of deal. You know, 10 minutes for $15 or something like that?

Um, maybe, I don't know.

Matthew Barrett

FRANK: I'm a banker who recently suffered a professional setback, and wondering whether I should retire.

Love Tarot Ricki: Was this directly related to two people?

Yeah! There was one person who decided whether the deal would go ahead, then there was the other guy I was going into business with.

The question is whether you should retire? Well, you're at a place when you can?

Freedom 55 is just a year away.

Are you also sensing that if you go forward there's a chance you'll suffer more reversals?

No. I'm more worried that my wife will drive me crazy.

[LAUGHS] You have so many interests, Matthew, I doubt that will happen.

What do you see?

I see the Tower in your future position There's an indication that your

world is going to get rocked . . .

Oh, oh!

. . . be it by retiring or not. After that it shows that you have the Nine of Pentacles, that talks about money, stability, and your secure home. Were you planning on travelling when you retire?

Sure. Absolutely. My wife is a few years younger than me and she's reaching her peak

while I'm reaching for the Viagra, if you know what I mean? What kind of problems do you see with that?

She's a very strong woman. What's her birthday?

April 27th.

Oh, yeah, she must drive you crazy! There's no way you can stop her from hitting her peak and it doesn't look like you want to. Can I speak freely?

Sure.

She likes to complain. She's going to complain whether you're working or not – that's not going to change. Even though you like what you do, you feel locked into it, and this is going to free you up to be the man inside that you haven't been allowed to be.

So I should just go with it?

Everything indicates that it's a good choice. It doesn't look like you're going to gain that much by waiting.

Did she marry me for my money?

What's her name dear?

Anne Marie.

Let's say, not just for your money. It's a factor. To say your money wasn't a factor would be a lie.

I guess I just feel a little insecure because her last boyfriend was a Saudi Arabian arms dealer and had considerably more money than I do.

But she didn't like him. That relationship would have been more for money than this one. She didn't like him and didn't like herself for being with him. He's left her with a real creepy feeling.

Yeah. I always thought Adnan was a prick.

William Thorsell

Psychic Lora: I see a legal matter you will fight to get money from, William. It's coming in the next year, you will gain from it. The negativity

of people I feel. You have good luck from God, but bad luck from people who will always put obstacles in your way of moving ahead. Your auras are very weak, and the positive energy around you is very weak as well. The man that I'm feeling around you in your work, that has negativity, is not going to go away. This person will always be this way and things are going to get a lot worse before they get better.

FRANK: Eek.

Are you having verbal disagreements with this man?

He's my boss. He doesn't like me. Do you see me getting fired? Because I can't even do this job well, to be honest.

I don't feel you'll stay in this work.

Oh, oh. Do you see where?

It will be where you are, around where you are, but it won't be in the work you're doing now. And the negativity will get stronger, I do feel that. 'Cause the negativity of this man is going to get worse.

Bastard.

Brian Orser

FRANK: I'm involved in a palimony suit and I'm wondering whether I should settle out of court.

Looking Beyond Psychics, Skye: Palimony, huh? Now that is what type of . . . ?

It's kind of like alimony, except there's no, you know, kids.

You mean just for being in a relationship with each other, no kids involved? What's your first name?

Brian.

What is your partner's name?

Michael.

Okaay. What I want you to do is focus in on Michael's voice. And what you're doing is creating a signal for me to tune into, much like a dolphin tuning into sonar. When you feel that signal strong and clear I need you to say his name out loud, with your

name, three times slowly, just concentrating on what his voice sounds like. Michael, Brian, Michael, Brian, Michael, Brian . . .

And your question is?

Should I settle this palimony thing out of court?

Is that what you want to do?

I'm a professional skater and I'm worried about what my fans will think if this continues to be dragged through the press. I don't know: am I even really gay? I saw Katrina's *Playboy* spread.

I'm glad you brought that up, because that's what I'm reading in your energy field.

Has my friend Mark 88Tewkesbury called?

No. Uh-uh.

Oh, he recommended you.

How wonderful! Tell him thanks very much for the referral.

Evan Solomon

James: What made you call today?

FRANK: I wrote a pretty shitty book. It's called *Crossing the Distance*, if you can believe it. It'll be published next year and I'm afraid everybody will see I'm a no-talent phoney.

You wrote a book? It's called Trust?

No, *Crossing the Distance*.

C-r-o-s-s-i-n-g the Distance. Okay. What does it deal with?

It's a novel.

And you want to know how it's going to do?

Yeah, I feel it's going to expose me for not being as talented as everyone thinks. And I mean, everyone.

Expose you.

Yeah. I'm worried I'm going to end up like . . . like Daniel Richler.

I don't know who that is.

See?

Well, if they didn't like it they wouldn't publish it. They'd only want a winner. Is there anything else you're questioning?

It's all got to do with this book. Everyone sees me as being this hip, young, next thing and really all I want is the house in Forest Hills and a Beemer in the driveway.

Well, there's nothing wrong with that.

No? No, I guess not. Thanks James, you really helped me out!

FRANK PRANKS

(March 10, 1999)
Black Beauty, Kiddie Porn?

The BC court's ruling on child pornography gave us pause: how far, we wondered, would some MPs be willing to go in order to curry favour with stone-cold stupid, family-values nutbars? As far as those two pages in the next issue are blank, we wagered.

To test our theory, we launched Families United for Canadian Kids – FUCK for short – and scoured classics of kiddie lit for choice inoffensive bits at which to take ridiculous offence. Then, posing as Reuter's intrepid Dougald Currie, we called a number of duly-elected elected doozies to find out what they made of FUCK's agenda. Let's listen in, shall we?

FRANK: Hi, I'm Dougald Currie, with Reuters, working on a story about Families United for Canadian Kids. Have you heard of them?

Myron Thompson (Ref-Wild Rose): It seems to ring a bell. Families United for Canadian Kids? I just can't place it or why, but it rings a bell.

They've been growing since the kiddie porn ruling in BC. I've been speaking to the President, Steve Collins, and he tells me they're in the process of enlisting the support of MPs. You haven't been approached, have you?

No, not at this point.

They're targeting certain children's books they feel are insidious or sexually suggestive. Not overtly pornographic like *Lolita* or anything, but classics they nevertheless want to do away with. What's your reaction to something like that?

Lemme tell you, I was a principal of a school for 15 years, and one of the things I always had in place when books came in was to screen them carefully and clear out all the trashy stuff that had no purpose in our library.

What kind of books did you throw out?

I don't even know if I could tell you one. But I know we did.

Let me tell you about a few of the

books F.U. has suspicions about. Several are by Maurice Sendak, including one called *In the Night Kitchen*. Collins said in an interview: "Even a Freudian would know there's something fishy about a story featuring a naked boy who gets baked in a pie and eats his way out."

Whuh! Now you're getting into the context. The title doesn't tell you much, does it?

Another is *Black Beauty*. Collins says the book draws attention to the colour of "Beauty" and how our

culture still, unfortunately, objectifies Negroes as sexual animals.

You mean *Black Beauty*, the story about the horse?

Yeah, the horse. He thinks it's where the expression "hung like a" comes from.

Ah, no, that's getting a little carried away. My initial thoughts? I say wait a minute here. There's been a movie and all that. It's a book about a horse. You can get a little paranoid about some of this stuff.

FRANK: So, have you heard about Families United for Canadian Kids?

Randy White (Ref-Langley-Abbotsford): I believe I just got a letter from them, if it's the same group, on child pornography.

Oh really? They've been getting quite a lot of support since that controversial ruling in BC.

Yeah.

One of the books they've singled out is *The 500 Hats of Bartholomew Cubbins* by Dr. Seuss. Collins says, "It might sound harmless, but a 'hat' was a common wartime slang for a prophylactic. What Dr. Seuss was actually telling children was, 'It's all right, kids, go ahead and have multiple sex partners. There's no consequences.' Of course we know differently today."

I thought I knew all Dr. Seuss books, but I don't know that one! I read Dr. Seuss to my kids and never had a problem. *The Cat in the Hat* comes to mind.

Ivan Grose (L-Oshawa): What's the name of the organization again?

FRANK: Families United for Canadian Kids.

[HEAVY SIGH] Oh, yeah.

You've heard about them? Their president, Steve Collins, is interested in targeting certain children's story books.

Yeah, I remember reading something about him.

What do you remember?

I've been through this before, where zealots get on school libraries. At one time it was *Little Red Riding Hood*. During the McCarthy era, it was a Communist book. Jesus Murphy!

He's after some well-known books by Dr. Seuss, Maurice Sendak –

Oh, Jesus! He's probably on the Jerry Falwell bandwagon, too, about the purple animal on TV that's gotta be homosexual because he's purple.

Listen to this quote from my interview with Collins: "We all know gay men frequent parks at night for anonymous anal sex, they quaintly call it 'cruising.' We're afraid of a title like this. It promises that wonder and mystery in a garden well past a child's bedtime will kindle a desire for perverse sexual experimentation in late adolescence. We need to nip this in the bud, so to speak.

We need to teach them the garden is poisonous before we raise another generation of nocturnal homosexual predators."

This guy is beyond help. Good God! Anal sex in parks? I never understood it got that blunt. Oh, Jesus. I'm speechless. Oh, my, my, my! I'm so baffled by what you've just read me. Were you solicited by him?

Er, yeah. I just wanted to see what kind of support he had.

Quite frankly, in the government caucus, he would have the obvious four who vote for the strangest things.

Frank: Who would that be?

Come on, you know who they are! Dan McTeague, Albina Guarnieri, Rosemary Ur . . . whose the other one? Anyways, they consistently vote against the government on anything that's weird.

FRANK: Have you heard about Families United For Canadian Kids?

Mac Harb (L – Ottawa Centre): No, not much.

But you have heard about them?

Yes.

They're concerned about Rudyard Kipling's *How the Camel Got its Hump*. They worry kids will snicker in the library when the title comes up; that it'll distract more sober-minded kids, and implant in their little minds a sexual curiosity which clamours for legitimate sex education.

Yes. Ah . . . arrrr, uhm. There's been a historic debate in this country, and I would say all across North America – [ORATION EXCISED ON ACCOUNT OF INDIFFERENCE.]

Yes, well another concern is that parents don't know these books exist in the schools, that it's the schools that use taxpayers money to bring the stuff in. Are you a parent?

Yes I am. *

Do you have any concerns about certain books your child might read?

Absolutely! I make sure, personally, to glance through the book first before I pass it on to her.

How old is she?

Two and a half. *

What about books that are sexually suggestive? Another one FU has a problem with is *The Vacillations of Poppy Carew*. He says that adolescent girls are too young to be vacillating.

Oh! Oh, my dear!

He wonders why they should be reading about it, since once a girl starts vacillating, it's hard to get her to stop.

Well, that certainly does go over the edge.

WHERE THE WILD THINGS ARE

FRANK PRANKS

So there's nothing wrong with vacillating?
No, no! There is a problem!
What are some of the concerns you have with vacillating girls?
What d'you mean? With vacillating girls?
Well, when I mentioned the title –
Oh! No! I haven't read it. If it's suggestive, then it deserves to be examined.
(* Ed. note: Congratulations, you're a dad! In the last federal election, Mac steadfastly refused to publicly acknowledge his parenthood, though rumours of a child, and speculation as to mom's identity, were in heavy rotation. The exploding cigar's on us.)

Bill Vankoughne (Ontario PC, MPP Frontenac-Addington): This type of thing should be looked at very seriously and frowned upon. If they bring it to my attention I'll certainly lend my weight through whatever it means.
FRANK: Collins has a problem with *The 500 Hats of Bartholomew Cubbins*, a book by Dr. Seuss. Let me read you a quote from my interview with him: "It might sound harmless, but a "hat," was a common wartime slang for a condom . . ."
I'd look at things like this and lend my support to people more versed in the problem and certainly bring it to the authorities' attention.
I don't want to let the cat out of the hat before he's spoken to you, but one of the things Mr. Collins mentioned is that he might be approaching sympathetic MPPs and MPs like you, to see whether you'd lend your support to their campaign, maybe allow him to put your name on their letterhead.
Certainly, once I learn a bit more about them. Of course, these are issues that should be supported. Anything we can do to discourage any type of information that might be impressionable on young people in
the wrong context. *(Ed. note: In May, 1996, Vankoughnet was arrested by Metro Toronto Flatfeet for soliciting an undercover police-woman. He pleaded guilty and was sentenced to hard labour in John School.)*
FRANK: Could you see making this a campaign promise, to get rid of these kind of books?
I see nothing wrong with it.

FRANK: What do you think about a book featuring a character named Dildo Buggers?
Darryl Stinson (Ref-Okanagan-Shuswap): That tweaks my interest to see . . . you know . . . whether it's a foreign title and that it is a legitimate name. As I understand those two words, I have a little bit of concern. I don't understand why they'd have a children's book with a name like that in it.
He's also concerned about *The 500 Hats of Bartholomew Cubbins*, by Dr. Seuss. Let me read you a quote from my interview with Collins: "It might sound harmless, but a "hat," was a
common wartime slang…"
"A hat?" . . . I'm 53-years-old and I've heard it used like he's talking about maybe once in my lifetime, maybe twice, I'm trying to recall now. My understanding is that a hat goes on my head. In England they call it a lid. We can't start changin' cultured words and that.
Some pornography researchers have argued that reading *Playboy* in adolescence is a bit of a gateway into harder pornography. Collins feels another Dr. Seuss book, *Hop on Pop*, is a not so subtle invitation to pedophilia because part of the text reads, "I like to hop on pop. Hop, hop, hop on pop." This he believes should be lighting up every parent's kiddie-porn radar because it could be leading a kid to pedophilia at a very early age.
As soon as I finish talking with you I'm going to be getting hold of some of these groups to see if they've had any contact in regards to this issue, and these books.

FRANK: He has a problem with *The Hobbit*, whose main character is called Dildo Buggers. Are you aware of the book?
Jim Gouk (Ref-West Kootenay-Okanagan): Vaguely.
He thinks it'll pervert children's minds.
Is that like if you play records backwards you'll hear satanic messages? I don't know, he's got to show me some real proof. I've seen stuff in some of my schools, literature put out by the gay community, and some of it was pretty unreal. It was explicit sexual content, how to play with your toys and how to prepare someone's rear end to get reamed; when you whip someone you should take care to wash your whips. I gotta say, I have a real problem with that.
Huh. And, er, what junior high was that?

(May 5, 1999)
All Rise for Governor General Jag Bhaduria

As dozens of Canadians begin wondering if anyone can fill the fuzzy slippers of Romeo LeBlanc, FRANK commissioned Charlie Powers of Decimal Research (a division of Frankland Capital Corp.) to sound out our nation's worthies. Visible minorities, risible women, and those with impaired perspective to the front of the class.

FRANK: We've been commissioned by the Prime Minister's Office to sound out possible candidates as to their interest in the position of Governor General.

Al Waxman: One hundred percent! And I'm prepared to say I love my country un l'océan à l'autre.
So you're bilingual?
I would be. I'd spend some time getting into it. Presumably you're given some notice?
Absolutely. How do you think your role as King of Kensington would be an asset to the position?
The thing I'd say about the King is that it undeniably touched a chord across the country. For a show in Canada to do that requires universality. To bridge the gaps across the country, to reach across barriers – [STUMPING CONTINUES AT LENGTH].
Is there anything that could bring disrespect to the office of the Queen's representative?
In my life? I think not.

Okay. So no history of marijuana?
Woo-aah! No. Er, well, I did partake a little during the 60s.
Would you be willing to travel to Nunavut?
In a minute!
In the last year or so, His Excellency has remodeled Rideau Hall in a high rococo style. Could you live with that?
Everywhere my wife and I have lived we've turned into a house of love. All I know, in response to your first question, would I be interested? The answer is 100%! I think it is important the country feels that kind of closeness that I would represent. That, "Hey, he's one of us!"

FRANK PRANKS

FRANK: What do you know about the office of the Vice-Regent?

Rita McNeil: Not a great deal to be very honest with you, Charlie, no. I'd have to sit and think about it all.

Yes . . .

One thing the Prime Minister has told us is he has a secret desire to record a duet with you of "The Wind Beneath my Wings."

[CHUCKLES] That's quite charming.

Have you heard Mr. Chrétien sing? He does a mean rendition of "When Irish Eyes are Smiling."

No, can't say that I have.

Are you politically active?

I have my political beliefs, but I certainly have done things for everybody, really.

Are you familiar with your Member of Parliament?

Oh, yes.

Who is it?

[CLICK.]

Hello? Miss McNeil??

[Charlie Powers waits a couple of minutes before redialing.]

I'm sorry about that. [NERVOUS LAUGHTER.] I have two Yorkies. They were jumping all over me and got caught up in the [phone] cord.

No problem. Is there anything in your past that could embarrass the Prime Minister? For instance, have you ever smoked marijuana?

No, none at all. Nothing that would be earth shattering.

Good to hear, ma'am. You were saying before, you know your MP quite well?

Yes, ah, Mr. Manning. Mr. Manning MacDonald.*

Have you ever had any association with the Communist Party?

No, no.

Have you ever heard of an Ezra Levant?

No, no; I'm sorry, I haven't.

One last question. To facilitate the selection process, would you be interested in donating to the Liberal Party of Canada?

Ah, I'd have to think that one over.

Sure.

A search of the Directory of Members reveals no such person.

FRANK: Your name has been put forward as a possible candidate.

Jag Bhaduria: Are you joking or what?

Would it be fair to characterize your relationship with the Prime Minister as "rocky"?

Rocky?! A gentleman should give a person a chance before hanging him out to dry.

Mr. Chrétien has expressed an eagerness to let bygones be bygones. And the public wants someone who is different

But Jag Bhaduria? The man who wants to turn the whole thing upside down?

Is there anything in your past that could bring the office into disrepute?

No, it's been a most impeccable record! Except fighting against racial discrimination as a result of which I wrote a letter. I'm not Jesus Christ; I'm not Mahatma Gandhi. I did write a letter . . .

May I ask the title of the last Canadian book you read?

Ah, um, I've read quite a few. Which was the last I don't know. My home library is filled with books.

Who is your favourite author?

Salman Rushdie. My heroes are those who have gone through inquisitions and that's where I survive.

Do you have a certain affinity with Rushdie?

Definitcly! I'm going through the same thing. Actually one of my books should be out soon: *Rushdie, Bhaduria and Persecution*.

Really? What are some of the points of the book?

He's a fighter, I'm a fighter; he's not given up, I've not given up. The Toronto [School] Board has put a headcount on my head to kick me out of town. They just hate my guts for the last 30 years. They're still persecuting me. The only difference between Jag Bhaduria and thousands of others is that they have given up. They've had nervous breakdowns, mental problems, hospitalization. Me, I'm stronger now than 10, 20 years ago . . . *[Complete rant available upon request.]*

Quickly, moving on, is there anyone you think would make a good Governor General?

Well, let's see. Elijah Harper, but he drinks too much. If you really want to look, and it must be, oh, one of them, is, um, er, oh gee. He was Chief of First Nations –

Mercredi?

Mercredi! Oh, ya, Ovidee! Good friend of mine.

If it's any help, I hear there are lots of teaching jobs available.

They won't take Jag Bhaduria, because you were kicked out of Toronto Board for being "incompetent." My competence is unparalleled in this country in physics. But life goes on and probably it will haunt them down the road. This man we persecuted but today he's still here, or wherever he is. I'll make my mark. Some read history, some write history, but I will make it!

Ovide Mercredi: Can you disclose who put my name forward? FRANK: Jag Bhaduria. He said he was a good friend of yours.

Oh, I see. Hmmm. *[Asks that we call him back when he is not on a cell phone.]*

[Later]: **It's hard to believe the Prime Minister would want me.**

I'm unaware of Mr. Chrétien's personal feelings. I've been asked to sound out candidates from outside politics.

Some political hacks don't work out, but the current one is good. To me we should try and find someone who is kind, who is good to people. That's one thing I'll say about him.

What do you think you could bring to the position?

I think for one thing – I hope I'm not wrong on this – but for the better part, people respect me; not just aboriginals. My community would be happy if I was appointed.

What kind of salary expectations would you have? Right now the salary is $98,000 tax free with free room and board and extensive use of the Lear Jet.

A Lear Jet? He, he, he! I make a lot of money right now, what I'm doing.

But the salary sounds okay, or is it too big a step down?

Yes, that would be a step down.

Even if it is tax free?

Yes.

Is there anything about your past that could potentially embarrass the Prime Minister?

I had problems in relation to my first marriage.

There wouldn't be any – I'm sorry, I have to ask this – problems with mari-

juana, gambling debts, unpaid taxes?

No, even when I was national Chief, I was very careful never to go to a casino. I'm not an alcoholic; I don't drink at all. As for marijuana, I've seen it in terms of gatherings, you know, university days. If this interview goes beyond this discussion, what happens? Are you going to call me back?

Yes. You'd probably have an informal meeting with Eddie Goldenberg. You have no problem with Eddie, do you?

No, none whatsoever. I've met him a few times.

What's the cause of the problems with Mr. Chrétien?

I didn't have a good relationship with his buddy, Ron Irwin. I don't know what he put in his mind, but I think a lot of it has to do with him. All I've heard is that I'm not on his list of favourite people.

If it's any consolation, I read something about how Ron Irwin isn't working out so well in Ireland.

[LAUGHS HEARTILY] I didn't think he'd do very good.

FRANK: We're just sounding out your interest in being the next Governor General.

Adrienne Clarkson: I'm sorry, I don't know who you are and I won't comment until I hear from somebody and have gotten some recommendation that I should speak with you in any way.

Yes, well, I hope you understand that I have been commissioned by the PMO –

By who? Percy Down? By who? Eddie.

Eddie Goldenberg? Well, I'll speak with Eddie then I'll speak with you. Okay, we'll take it from there then.

Yes, I will speak with Eddie. Yes, I will speak with Eddie tomorrow [CLICK].

FRANK: What do you think you could bring to the office of Governor General?

Gerald Regan: I'm sorry, Mr. Powers, you have me wordless.

Before I take your name to the next stage, one thing I'm asking all candidates is whether there's anything in their past that could potentially embarrass the Prime Minister.

Yup. Well, let me think about this and I'll call you back.

Hey, wait a second. You're not that Gerald Regan, are you?

FRANK PRANKS

(January 26, 2000)

Bernie Earle, We Hardly Knew Ya!

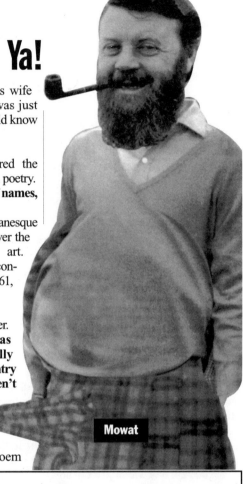

Mowat

Heritage Moment: A slow news week in a cold, barren land blessed only with an overabundance of name-dropping literary pseuds. Counting our blessings, we invent an obscure Canadian poet, Bernie Earle. Ten minutes later, we kill him off, and start calling around for the inevitable glowing tributes. Bernie, we hardly knew ye.

Hi this is Alan Martin calling from the *National Post* . . .

Farley Mowat: WHAAAT??!! The NATIONAL POST! I thought I was proscribed in the *National Post* . . . heh heh heh.

FRANK: I take no responsibility for the editorial board . . . I'm calling about Bernard Earle, the Canadian poet who died yesterday.

Never heard about him.

One of the reasons I'm calling you, other than you being a literary giant, is that his last words he told his wife were, "Farley Mowat," and I was just wondering whether you would know what that was about?

Give me his name again?

Bernard Earle, he's considered the Charles Bukowski of Canadian poetry.

With my fabulous memory of names, I can't spot it.

He was a kind of Andy Kaufmanesque personality, used to do these over the top pieces of performance art. Maybe you might recall his confrontation with Sylvia Plath in 1961, down at upstate New York. . . ?

Oh ya!

. . . where he sucker-punched her.

Yeah? You can quote me as saying the loss of any really outrageous writer in this country is a terrible disaster. There aren't enough of us.

He often used to run afoul with the Ontario Human Rights Commission, like he did in 1994 for his poem

Obituary of Bernie Earle, 1921-2000

*P*rolific Canadian poet Bernie Earle, "the bard of the beer parlour," has died in a supermarket mishap in Mississauga, Ont.

Mr. Earle is perhaps best known for his 120-page epic poem, "Ladies & Escorts Only," with its oft-quoted opening lines, "They piss you off, them Sunday blue laws, / No rye, no draft, no nuthin'," for which he was a highly unpopular choice for the Governor General's Award for English poetry in 1955.

Mr. Earle's other major works include *Ode on a Grecian Urinal* (1959), *The Love Song of Lorne "Gump" Worsley* (1966), *Let Us Compare Thingies* (1969), *The Rejected Poems of Bernie Earle, 1947-72* (1972), *Death of a Girly Man* (1977), and *A Wide Peculiar Boy* (1989). In all, he published more than 200 volumes of verse.

Throughout Mr. Earle's long career, critics were divided over the worth of his work. Some praised it as a defiant testament to the quotidian lives of ordinary Canadians, while others, like Northrop Frye, called it "a grating screech of inanity from the bottom of a dirty beer glass."

Saint Bernard (Bernie) Earle — his parents wanted a dog — was born to a family of Mimico, Ont., chinchilla ranchers in 1929. "Them sure was hungry times," Mr. Earle told biographer Dougald Currie in 1991, "but at least we was warm."

A Grade 3 dropout, Mr. Earle once described his method of writing as "drinking till I'm totally shit-faced, and then just scribbling till I puke."

Controversy dogged Mr. Earle

"A friggin Towel Head Drove Me to the Wrong Address." Does this ring any bells for you?

[LAUGHS] No, but it sounds good though, I like it. How many of us would dare say that?

Getting back to his last words, saying Farley Mowat, what do you make of that, did you ever meet him?

I can't recall it, but I can suspect that he's hoping that I'll see to it that his memory, no not his memory, what, that his legacy, that he isn't forgotten, and that his likes do not vanish from the face of the earth!

Coren

That sounds appropriate enough. Any other comments you would like to pass on to the *National Post*, or Ken Whyte perhaps?

I do hope he took a run at Conrad Black.

Well, between you and me, he was known for calling him a "son of a bitch."

Well, you can quote me as saying that

Conrad Black will miss him deeply. **Michael Coren: I'm not sure you have the right person, though. Why me in particular?**

FRANK: After the beer parlour years, Mr. Earl became a born-again Christian in '87 and he'd talk about bringing faith into the secular arena of public debate.

You know, I wish I could be helpful, but I just know so little. I'm not really the right person. Who else have you tried? I might be able to give you some names, though.

We spoke to Mordecai Richler and we're trying to get through to Adrienne Clarkson, uh, Farley Mowat, Timothy Findley . . .

Yeah, the heavy hitters. I know so little I really wouldn't know what to say.

Did you ever see him read?

Bernard Earl?

Yeah.

I don't think I've even heard of him, I'm sorry to be so naive.

"Ladies and Escorts Only?"

Forgive me, but no.

Okay, I'm terribly sorry.

No, not at all, but, I, I thought you might have meant Bernie Kerr when you first said it. I'm obviously showing ignorance here, but I don't know. Who's Bernie Kerr?

Oh, he's just a friend of mine. I thought you might have been talking about him. A couple of weeks ago he died, but . . . I'm sorry I can't be more helpful. This is a Canadian author?

Yeah, a poet. I'm still sort of working through the notes here but he was either nominated for or actually won the Governor-General's award for English poetry in 1955.

Oh. I wasn't even born then, save in this country. What does it say in the — what-do-you-call-it, the list of Canadian writers and so on?

I don't even have that entry handy. I've just got some bio notes.

Uh, let's have a look here for you. Which company did you say you were from?

Uh, from CP.

[FLIPPING OF PAGES AND THOUGHTFUL NOISES] Hmm. It's not even listed in the . . . E-A-R-L?

Yeah, or maybe with an E on the end?

There's no listing in the *Companion*

---

throughout his career, not only for his unabashed reliance on the English vernacular, but his abrasive personality. He gained particular notoriety for sucker-punching American poet Sylvia Plath during a poetry symposium sponsored by the State University of New York, Buffalo, in 1961. "She was such a wet blanket, that gal. I was just trying to loosen her up a bit," he said at his trial.

As recently as 1994, Mr. Earle came under fire from the Ontario Human Rights Commission for his collection of Petrarchan sonnets, "A Friggin' Towel-Head Drove Me to the Wrong Address."

Mr. Earle was married six times and fathered nine children, although none with any of the women he was married to. He once opined, "I guess there's just something about being married to me makes it so's I can't stand them no more."

In 1962, he won the Lorne Pierce Medal for Literature for his found poem, "Public Eviction Notice."

In 1972, after consuming several kilograms of sauerkraut, pickled eggs, and baked beans, and several kegs of draft beer, he performed, for the one and only time, his pro-Vietnam-War sound poem, "Here Comes the Stone Age," with the

Edmonton Symphony Orchestra.

A decade-long experiment with concrete poetry ended in 1974, when he sustained a double hernia trying to write "Bring back Dow Kingsbeer / I really miss it" in cement blocks on his front lawn.

Mr. Earle was also the author of several lightly regarded novels and a volume of memoirs entitled *I'm a Big, Fat Fake*. The latter earned him the Leacock Medal for humour in 1968, an honour he refused to accept. "It's not funny," he said. "I'm being dead serious here."

FRANK PRANKS

to Canadian Literature . . . Maybe I'm not as embarrassed as, as I was. I was fairly familiar with Canadian literature even earlier on, but that name . . .

He's the one who hit Sylvia Plath. Does that ring a bell?

Well, that's a very, very good thing to do, and I have read of someone hitting Sylvia Plath, but that name really means nothing to me, I'm so sorry, especially since the guy is dead. Let's have a look and see if there's anything else I can help you with . . . [MORE SCHOLARLY RUSTLING] Let's have a look at [UNINTELLIGIBLE]

Sorry, what's the book you're using? We've probably got one around here somewhere . . .

Uh, there's a few here . . . *Oxford Companion to Canadian Literature* . . . *Dictionary of Canadian Quotations* . . . um, have you looked him up on the Internet?

Uh, I haven't, no. They've just given me this list of people to contact.

It's not in the book of quotations. I suppose the only reason they would have given you my name perhaps, is that I was working on a biography of Mordecai.

Oh.

Because otherwise I really have very little qualification in this area . . . but no, the books I have don't mention him, so I'm sorry I can't be more helpful.

Oh, that's all right. So, there's no entry at all there?

In the *Oxford Companion to Canadian Literature* I couldn't see one, nor in the *Dictionary of Canadian Quotations*, and there are more esoteric books, but. . . .

Hold on, there's probably a list of Governor-General's winners here. So you say it was for poetry in the 50s?

Yes, that was his debut, but I think he published right into the early 90s.

Well, going back to . . . um . . . okay [MORE SHUFFLING] . . . it's very

odd that I wouldn't have heard of him at all if he was still publishing in this decade . . . hmmm . . . 1950 . . . In the 1950s you say he won the G-G for poetry?

I don't know if he won it . . .

Winning it isn't that impressive, being nominated is bare-ly worth a mention, I would have thought. I can't see him. I've been looking at the list here . . . Bernard Earl . . . I can't see the name . . . My gosh. Pierre Berton in '56 . . . for non-fiction. Amazing. [ON AND INTER-MINABLY ON]

FRANK: He was the author of "Ladies & Escorts Only."

Inky Mark (Ref = Heritage Critic): I think I've heard the title.
Yeah?

I've never read it, though.
It was up for a Governor-General's Award for Canadian poetry in '55, so it's a bit of a trivia question. He's also a bit of an anomaly in that he very proudly pointed to the fact that he never once took a government grant for his work.

Back in those days there probably weren't any — were there any grants to be had back then? I don't know.
I don't believe that the support was quite as generous as it is today, but he published well into the early 90s, never to any great recognition. But, uh, Mr. Manning was apparently a fan of Mr. Earl's work. It was very much about Canadian self-reliance and individual-ism. So you think you may have heard about "Ladies & Escorts Only?"

I've heard the title, but I didn't know what it was.
He won a Lorne Pierce Medal in '62 for "Public Eviction Notice," a found

poem. He was a bit of an odd character but very independent.

These are the kind of people we need to model after, who, you know, are independent and can do things for themselves, you know, without, without, reaching out to the pockets of government. I guess, as critic, all I can say is, I guess, applaud his efforts, in, uh, doing what he had done for the country, and being a marquee poet, who like many of our mar-quee individu-als, Canadians don't know about. I guess he'd fall in that category, like many of our war he-roes and other writers, but certainly his abilities to do things for himself, uh, stand out as well. Certainly, what a contrast to the 90s, you know? Some in this country think you can't succeed without the government throwing money at it.
His wife, Susan Musgrave, said, and this is preliminary, but apparently his last words were "Inky Mark."

Whaa?
That's partly why we're calling you.

Well, I'm, uh, surprised. To hear he echoed . . . you're sure that's what he said, eh?
Yeah, and she didn't know who you were.

Well, then, he must have followed the news clippings because I'm the arts critic as well, I've held the port-folio over the last couple of years, so that's how he probably heard about me. Maybe he read some of the things I've said regarding govern-ment's role in the funding of arts

and, uh, entertainment. I think we all believe that. I know as a teacher I believe in development and support but there's a limit to that, too. I think you'll have to phone the wife later on and see if she knows any more about it. I'd be interested to know. I'd like to send them a sympathy card.

Susan Musgrave (poet and wife of bank robber-cum-author Stephen Reid): Bernard Earle? Never heard of him.

FRANK: Well, there're two reasons why you might have heard of him. The first is because he was considered the Charles Bukowski of Canadian poetry; and secondly, it appears he was an early drinking buddy of your husband Stephen Reid.

Sorry, I'd like to think I know most of the poets in this country, but that's really odd, I don't recall him.

They seem to have had a falling out somewhere along the way, but he reviewed *Jack Rabbit Parole* for the Kingston *Whig Standard*, where he was quoted as calling Stephen "a gun-toting cry baby." Would you know what that was about?

No, you say he's a poet?

Yes.

Well, I never saw a review that called him a gun-toting cry baby either, cause I don't think that was what he was or is.

You don't think they did any time together? Maybe robbed a bank together or something?

No. I've been writing poetry for 30 years, not that that means I've never heard of somebody, but we must have moved in different circles. Did he publish at all, was he a street poet?

His work was considered in some circles as a defiant testimony to the everyday lives of ordinary Canadians, while others, like Northrop Frye, called it "a grating screech of inanity

from the bottom of a dirty beer glass."

Oh, that's why I've never heard of him, there are a lot of poets like that that never go into print as much. Sometimes they distribute their work on street corners . . .

No, he was quite prolific. He even won a Gov. Gen's award for poetry in 1955 . . .

How quickly we are forgotten, eh. What kind of indictment of Canadian society is that?

I think it's like everything in society, there's too much of everything, we can't retain, remember . . . I mean the days of Keats and Shelley, there were hundreds of poets, but only a handful rose to the top . . . I know there a lot of poets on the fringe that I don't know about, but not usually the older ones. The name rings a bell, but I can't say I can think of any-thing he wrote.

Some of the things he wrote were *Death of a Girly Man* (1977), *A Wide Peculiar Boy* (1989). You never remember him coming over, hanging out with Stephen?

No, sorry.

FRANK: I'm just calling around to get some different reactions to the death of Bernard Earle, the Canadian poet who died yesterday. I was just wondering whether you would be able to add a few words to my story?

Bert Archer: Hmmm [PAUSE FOR A COUPLE SECONDS]. I'm not sure that I could. I'm not sure I

know enough about him to say anything.

Well one reason I'm calling you is that his wife told me that his last words were "Bert Archer."

What!?

Do you have any idea what the significance of that would be?

I have no idea. Yikes! When did he die? Well that's enormously interesting. I don't have any idea why he would have said that.

Do you think that maybe he was passing on the torch to another generation?

Possibly, but I'm not a poet. Umm, aah, maybe if you wouldn't mind sending me by email some of the basic facts you have compiled so far, I would be able to look at that and make a comment, if you give me a couple of hours.

So you have no recollection of his legacy?

Not immediately, but, ah, perhaps with a little bit of thought I would be able to. So would you like my email? It's archer@istar.ca.

FRANK: Thanks very much.

FRANK: What are your recollections of Mr. Earle?

Jack Granatstein: I don't have any I'm afraid. I don't know who he is.

He was considered the Charles Bukowski of Canadian literature.

I'm, ah, an historian, sorry. What can I say? But for God's sake don't put me in as saying I never heard of the guy. That would be terrible.

He was an abrasive, foul mouthed character . . .

Obviously not of the areas I move in . . .

So you don't recall the dust-up he had with Sylvia Plath in 1961?

Oh, I'm sorry! I, I, thought you were trying to tell me he was a Canadian.

He is a Canadian. He was just down in New York state on a poetry symposium . . .

FRANK PRANKS

Oh, okay.

So you remember the time he sucker-punched Slyvia Plath?

Sorry, I thought you were talking about the husband of Slyvia Plath, whatshisname . . . I'm sorry I'm totally out to lunch here.

Steve Paikin: I think you have the wrong feller. Bernard Earle?

FRANK: He was considered the Charles Bukowski of Canada. He won the 1955 Gov Gen's award for Poetry. **You watch StudioII and you assume that I'm wonderfully literate, knowleageable about all things in the arts kind of a person, and I'm so sorry to let you down.**

So you have no recollection of his work from 1955, "Ladies & Escorts *Only?*"

Sorry. No.

Evan Solomon: Returning your call.

FRANK: Thanks. I'm just calling around to get some reaction to the death of Bernard Earle who died earlier this morning.

I can tell you I've been in studio all day and I did not know that had happened. I just got out of the studio.

What did you know about the guy?

You know, I'm, I'm not the guy to comment. I mean I know of my university days, my poetry reading, to be honest, is rather extensive but a lot of it is in American poets. But I'm probably not the guy.

Yeah, he was considered the Bukowski of Canada . . .

Off the record, honestly? Bukowski, not my kind of thing. I'm a John Ashbery, that kind of thing. I love Margaret Atwood's poetry. But Bukowski and the Beats, that just wasn't my type of thing. I'm not the greatest guy to comment on this. My producer might be better.

Yeah, but I was thinking you have a better public persona than your producer . . .

Yeah, I know.

What do you think about his legendary dust-up with Slyvia Plath?

I'm just not up on that. I'm reasonably ashamed to say that.

What do you remember hearing about Mr. Earle? Among his fans he counted people such as Mordecai Richler, Pierre Trudeau, Margaret Atwood, I even hear that Preston Manning was quite fond of his work.

I didn't know that Preston was a poetry reader. Again, the reason I'm being hesitant is that I don't like to comment on things that I'm not very well versed on. Cause then I get called in and basically get called a blowhard. Honestly, this is something I'm not an expert on.

Yeah, but you do have a fairly grounded reputation as a cultural commentator.

Yeah I know, but I'm not being evasive. If I had an opinion that I thought that anyone would care about, and I do, there are things that I'm very passionate about, as editor of *Shift*, or as a writer, obviously I'm engaged in the literary world, rather passionately, but this is something, you just told me he passed away, I hadn't even thought about it for five seconds. You know what I'm saying? I just walked out of my stu-dio. It's not that I have no comment. Obviously it's a loss for the Canadian literary world, and for Canadians, but these are the kind of bromides that are so unhelpful in these kind of situations.

Why don't you like that type of on-the-street, Beat writing?

It's just not the kind of poetry, the kind of poetry I read a fair bit of, is of a different nature. If you look at a guy like Erin Mouré, who's interested in language games, or even Margaret Atwood's poetry, or John Ashbery's poetry, or . . . it's a different school of poetry, that kind of different beat, that hard street, almost spoken word stuff has not been what does it for me. I feel I'm going to say something about this guy that's negative, and I have nothing negative to say about this guy. What I'm saying is that I don't feel anything. I'm not saying his work was unappealing or no good, none of that I'm saying. If I didn't like his work I would be more than willing to state my opinion. I'm dancing around here cause I might be the guy to talk about a lot of literary things, I've got a degree in English, but this is not one area.

What kind of work of his did you read at university?

I don't know.

Must have been one of those Friday morning classes.

It was just Canadian poetry. Who, what, are you calling from, the *Post*?

Yeah, I'm just doing a bit of freelance work for them.

How old was he?

Seventy-eight. He was a flamboyant guy: had about six marriages, nine kids from different woman . . .

I don't know this guy . . .

Some people praised his work as a defiant testimony to the everyday lives of ordinary Canadians, while others, like Northrop Frye, called it "a grating screech of inanity from the bottom of a dirty beer glass." There are definitely opinions out there about him.

Who else have you talked to about this?

Mordecai Richler, Farley Mowat. Farley was an old drinking buddy of his.

You caught me at a bad time here. I just got out of the studio, I'm just collecting my thoughts. I'm just trying to get on the web here to see about this event. Hold on a sec [TALKS TO HIS PRODUCER]. Talk to Stan Bevinton at Coach House. Call there and someone will give you Stan's number. My producer doesn't even know this guy. Listen, I'm so sorry that I have been so unbelieveably unhelpful to you.

Thanks, that's okay.

Isn't that wonderful that the host of a Canadian book show has no comment on that.

FRANK: I don't know whether you've heard yet but Bernard Earle, the Canadian poet, died this morning.

Jeannie Bekker: Oh, I didn't know. What's your reaction to the news?

I have to plead ignorance, I just don't know enough.

The reason I'm calling you is that he is said to have written a series of poems dedicated to you.

Oh, get outta here. Get outta town.

In one piece of work, he made several references to your "helacious falafel of a mouth." It seems that he was infatuated with you and was an incredible fan of *Fashion TV*. Did you ever meet him?

Jeannie

[LAUGHS LIKE A HYENA] That sounds wonderful, I mean that's a wonderful image, makes me want to go out and have Middle Eastern food tonight. Where did he live?

Missassauga.

Could you send a copy of the poem?

FRANK: Sure I could try. But since I have you on the phone, do you remember any of his outrageous public art performances in the '70's? One of the things he used to do, like Charles Bukowski, would be to get himself all liquored up then write till he puked. He once did a show at the O'Keefe Centre where he consumed several plates of sauerkraut, pickled eggs, baked beans and a bunch of beer, before performing his pro-Vietnam War poem, "Here Comes the Stone Age."

Oow-eee, mmmh. Really? How old was he when he died. I'd love to see his work.

How do you feel being the subject of his poetry?

I would be flattered being the subject of anyone's poetry. Why not? I think anyone would be flattered to be made reference to in any type of artistic endeavour, so long as it wasn't horrible defamatory. You want to be mused about. Why would anybody be flattered that their image made an impression on someone's

heart or mind, to whatever degree. The other thing that stood out was his legendary dustup with Sylvia Plath in 1961 . . .

Really?!

. . . where he suckerpunched her at a poetry symposium . . .

Hmmm. Really? I'd love to see some poetry, if you have it.

Half an hour later, Solomon calls again.

Evan Solomon: Hi, it's Evan Solomon here. I can't find anything about this on the wires. Tell me his name again?

FRANK: B-e-r-n-a-r-d E-a-r-l-e.

I have no clue who this guy is. Honestly, I thought you were referring to Earle Birney, who is dead . . .

Yeah, that was Bernie's biggest problem: he was always in the shadow of Earle Birney. But let me assure you they were very different.

I can tell you something, I have no clue who this guy is and I've been looking for it. My comments about are, at best, useless. Bernard Earle? I have no clue who this poet is.

That's okay.

You know, for a second I looked on the wire and I thought, "Is this a FRANK PRANK?"

I would be extremely surprised if it was.

No, no, I would be surprised too.

You're not with FRANK Magazine are you?

Oh, God no.

You know Noah Richler, you work with him?

Well, I know of him, but I'm a freelancer based out of Ottawa.

You know Noah Richler, you work with him?

Okay, I was just wondering. Look, I'm not

FRANK PRANKS

the guy to talk to about Bernard Earle.

FRANK: Okay.

Half an hour later, Solomon calls again.

Solomon: I have to bother you one last time, Evan Solomon. Nobody here has heard of Bernard Earle.

FRANK: Really?

I'm talking about NOOOBODY!

Well, I have a book of his poetry.

How do you spell his name?

B-e-r-n-a-r-d E-a-r-l-e.

It's not in the Canadian Biography, it's not on the web, it's not on Indigo. Everybody in the CBC has never heard about him, including the Kahunas.

Well, that's strange, cause I've talked to numerous people and got their reaction . . .

But it's not even on the wires . . .

That doesn't surprise me at all, he spent his last few years well below radar. He was very much a recluse.

Well, Earle Birney died in '95 . . .

Yeah, but we're talking about Bernard Earle.

A real guy, Bernard Earle, my God. You say he had a dustup with Sylvia Plath?

Yeah, it happened down at a poetry symposium in New York state in '61. One person I contacted said Bernie found her a bit uptight and thought he could loosen her up by sucker-punching her.

You've got me really intrigued, because I thought you were referring to Earl Birney, but I don't know anything about this guy. What's the name of one of his book?

Let's see, we've got *The Rejected Poems of Bernie Earl, 1947-72* (1972), then there was *Death of a Girly Man*, published in 1977 . . .

Death of a Girly Man? **Are you serious?**

Listen, I've talked to a lot of people about this

Jesus Christ.

The last collection was *A Wide Peculiar Boy*, published in 1989.

[WHISTLES] Wow.

I tell you he's been out there.

I don't wanna tell you about who I've asked about this, but people who are senior cultural people here, like well known people, have never heard of this guy.

He used to do some real Andy Kaufman-esque performance art.

Well, all right, I guess that's it. The more I looked, the more I realized I knew nothing about this guy, the more I thought this isn't the real deal, but now I'm intrigued to read about it. When's your article coming out? You talk to Mordecai about this?

Of course, Mordecai knows him from the 1940s, 1950s.

Really? Whad he say?

That he was a prolific drinker and a prolific writer, one of those guys who would sit at the table and get himself absolutely shitfaced then fall on the floor.

Really?

The guy also only had about a Grade 3 education, was very poor, came from a very small town, and worked his way up.

Okay, I look forward to reading about this obscure Canadian poet.

Irshad Manji: I've never heard about him, but I'm so not the right demographic.

FRANK: One of the reasons I'm calling you is that you have a rep for taking on white male dinosaurs around town . . .

Aaaww.

Are you familiar with Charles Bukowski, the American writer/poet who liked his booze and women?

No.

Anyhow, in 1994 Mr. Earle wrote a poem called "*A Friggin Towel Head Drove Me to the Wrong Address*," which got him in a bit of hot water with the Ontario Human Rights Commission.

[LAUGHS].

Does this ring any bells for you?

No, I must confess I have never heard of that poet or that poem. I'm completely ignorant, how's that for a quote. If using a word like Towel Head get's people talking, discussing, arguing, all of with some degree of thought, and that's what's he's known for, then that is a loss for Canadian literature.

(February 23, 2000)

Billion Dollar Boondoggle

There are up to three billion stories in the celebrated Human Resources Transitional Jobs Fund, so we didn't figure anybody would notice if we added a couple of our own. To test our hypothesis, we took on the Herculean task of making up fictional federal job creation scams more incredible than the real ones. Then, posing as reporters from the gutter press (Daily Tubby, Globe and Minion, *etc.*), we phoned MPs for expressions of predictable outrage.

Interesting footnote: Staff in Knee-Dip MP Michelle Dockrill's office informed our faux Daily Tubby reporter that she and other NDP caucus members had decided to give Conrad's organ the silent treatment until the increasingly ugly Calgary Herald strike gets resolved.

A Gilles Duceppe spokesthingy pissily informed us that the chief Blochead was disinclined to comment because of the lawsuit between his party and the Tubby re: misappropriation of funds allegations by the Post.

A shocked and appalled Dave Chatters (Ref-Athabasca), however, began frantically preparing Question period zingers based on our fictional job fund recipients.

Credulous NDP finance critic Lorne Nystrom did Chatters one better, issuing an urgent press release: "Conrad Black's Hollinger and Bank of Montreal Get Handouts!"

Enter the media. A pack o' hacks including Juliette O'Neil (Ottawa Petfinder), Stephen Thorne (CP) and Heather Scofield (Globe and Mail) descended on the story. At Lord Almost's flagship, crack investigative reporter Stewart Bell was hauled off the lesbian desk to record Hollinger's denials for the Saturday edition:

Hollinger VP Peter Atkinson refuted the allegations with the whopper that "No one at Hollinger has any interest in heraldry," and tacked on his patron's standard gust of libel chill: "[this] appears to be defamatory and we will seek the usual recourse."

In the end, the Tubby and the Petfinder went with the story, and we created a day's employment for several bored hacks at no additional cost to the taxpayer.

FRANK: I wanted to get your reaction to some Access to Information documents I've received concerning HRDC's job creation grants . . .
Dave Chatters (Ref-Athabasca): Oh ya.
One concerns a small textile manufacturer in your riding called Baba Ganouj Inc., which received $30,000 in 1998.

In my riding? I've never heard of them. Where are they located? Somewhere in Fort McMurray. **Oh, ya.**

I don't know how they could get much more crazier than funding Sikh terrorists or training Inuit to be lap dancers.

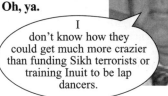
Chatters

They're apparently makers of fine turbans. **I'm not aware of the company. I'm not sure about the circumstances of the grant. The first question that comes to my mind is that unemployment in Fort McMurray is almost non-existent. The place is an absolute boom town because of the oil and gas industry. So how did they qualify?**
Well, this is one of the things I've been talking to my sources in CSIS about. They're saying that this company is actually a front for some Sikh extremists from the BC mainland, they've been using Fort McMurray cause it's kind of out of the way and all. Their application says they were going to hire 50 turban makers, but they only have 10 on staff.
Yeah, I would think a company as big as what they're talking about would be a little more visible, so I guess that fits with that. It certainly fits the profile of what's been happening with these transitional job funds, without qualifying and without application. So certainly, I would have concerns about that. We talked about this yesterday in caucus, that the first suggestion was that through Access to Information, we check in our own ridings to see what funds went where. You kind of jumped the gun on us on that one.
Yeah, it was a bit of a lucky thing for us. Do you think the Sikhs were taking advantage of your aboriginal constituents to infiltrate under the cover of darkness, so to speak?
Oh no, they couldn't do that.
How do you feel about them getting the money?
That would certainly be my question to Jane Stewart and the HRDC: how they geddit, when others that I thought were justified in asking, couldn't? We need

an answer to that. We've been accusing her all along of dispensing these funds where they are not qualified, simply for political reasons. With these allegations of impropriety around this company, it certainly raises all kinds of questions about how they would geddit.

What's your feeling about the government subsidizing the turban industry?

If it's a legitimate company and unemployment in the area is 12 percent or higher and they are proposing to create jobs, the program is there and if they qualify, my riding deserves those funds as much as any other in Canada. I'm not particularly excited about the program to begin with. I think there are better ways to address those things perhaps. It's borderlining on criminal to dispense those funds to companies and people who don't qualify. What was the name of the company again?

Baba Ganouj Inc.

Baba Ganouj Inc., that's a new one.

[Calls an hour later, leaves message]

Chatters: Hi Alan, it's Dave Chatters. I was just thinking about the issue we spoke earlier about. I checked and the company in fact doesn't have a phone number in Fort McMurray, and I checked with the Chamber of Commerce, they've never heard of the company. I then checked with the Municipal Business License office and no company can operate out of the municipality without a business license and they've never heard of them. Essentially, they do not exist in Fort McMurray. That might be of interest to your story. Please feel free to call me back. Thanks.

FRANK: Hi, Mr. Chatters. Thanks for calling back. The issues you raised are very interesting. There's another program that got some money in Nunavut

under somewhat similar circumstances — no address, no telephone number — and I just wanted to bounce that by you. They got $22,650 to train women in Nunavut as Lapp Dancers — that's weird, it's spelt L-A-P-P . . .

Chatters: Good God . . .

. . . I don't know what that's about, maybe it's some kind of cultural exchange. Anyways, the money went to a place in Iqaluit called the Polar Bare Bar . . . Jesus, that's spelt B-A-R-E . . .

Uh huh.

. . . no follow-up, no documentation about it. We called up to Iqaluit and there's no listing for the Polar Bare Bar.

Sure. But according to CSIS, this outfit in Fort McMurray does exist? They were investigating them?

Well, my source said that it's quite common for militant Sikhs from B.C. to go further north to escape the attention of the police, where they'd be below police radar. So that's why an organization like Baba Ganouj would go to a riding like yours.

It certainly raises a lot of questions. When you going to go with the story?

Probably, this weekend. We're doing a special on some of the more ludicrous recipients that got funding.

I'd like to ask Jane Stewart about it in Question Period on Monday, as long as you've gone with the story already. I don't want to upstage you on that one.

I appreciate that. What do you think about these programs. What the hell is going on?

I can help thinking that it's exactly what Diane [Ablonczy] said, it's simply money going to those favoured for political purposes. I don't know what else you can conclude when you see those kind of things. Either that or there's such bad control that anyone can get a

chunk of money. It has to be one or the other. I can't see how I could just call up HRDC and say I need $30,000 and receive it. There has to be some connection with someone in HRDC that cuts these cheques without even looking at them. It's really curious. I'm looking forward to the discussion and to getting to the bottom of it.

You've never seen the Lapp Dancers on tour have you?

Oh, definitely not. If they're lap dances in the conventional sense, I hardly think Canadian taxpayers' money should be going to train lap dancers. It's almost so absurd it's crazy.

Putting aside the financial aspect of this fiasco, what do you think the moral implications of that are?

Yeah, it's an absolute outrage. The moral implications of this are so outrageous that the public outrage over this, when it's exposed, will be as great, or greater, than the hockey player fiasco. It raises all kinds of images in the public's mind, but I don't think the ones you're talking about are so bizarre that they go even beyond what people think there might be.

So you think there might be even more crazier things?

Well, I don't know how they could get much more crazier than funding Sikh terrorists or training Inuit to be lap dancers. That's about as far off the beaten track as you can get, I should think.

Do you think the spelling L-A-P-P, might be a way to throw us off the scent?

Maybe, or maybe there's some Inuit or cultural significance that it means something else. But being that it's a bar, it makes you wonder. It really looks suspicious. You can't imagine a highly placed bureaucrat approving these. And of course, all

of these approvals had to have the minister's name on the bottom for it to go out. Whether the minister signed a bunch of papers without looking, I don't know. But surely, Pettigrew couldn't have signed them without seeing what the name was. To sign a $20,000 grant to a bar called the Polar Bare Bar. . . .

Do you think it's a linguistic thing, that Pettigrew just didn't get it?

I think you're being overly generous. I think all hell is going to break loose Monday when these questions are asked, especially after that little performance with Jane Stewart and Chretien yesterday. If there are any more developments or an aspect you'd like to hear the answer, to just give the office a call and we'll try and adjust the question to include it. But I'm going to go with this one in my riding, particularly because not that long ago I applied for a company in Slave Lake under that additional job fund and was turned down because they only had an unemployment rate of 10 percent, so I'm going to tie it to that.

FRANK: Calling to get your reaction to some Access to Information documents concerning the HRDC job fund.

Diane Ablonczy (Ref-Nose Hill): Okay.

Some of them are kinda crazy, but they might be of interest to you for Question Period next week. Supposedly, $52,750 went to something called the Diesel Dyke Project in Brantford—say,

This just blows me away!

isn't that Jane Stewart's riding? **Yeah.**

This program was to teach lesbians how to repair engines, the rationale was that lesbians need an alternative to the patriarchal, phallocentric methods of traditional auto mechanics.

Aw. The language suggests that this is more about political correctness than it is about job creation.

Yeah, in their application, they mention how they object to words likeMASTERcylinder, camSHAFT, STICKshift, connecting ROD, STROKE, TOOL, JACK and MANifold — words that they see as misogynist or otherwise objectionable . . .

I would say that Canadian's money should be about helping people work, not about pursuing political agendas.

Have you heard about any other programs like this?

No, this just blows me away. It's so obviously designed as a political agenda that, [SIGHS], it even surprises me. Can you send me that doc?

Sure, do you have a fax number.

Yeah, send it to 2-5 . . . , shoot, how many times do I fax myself . . . ? 992-2537. I'd appreciate that. We're going to have a strategy meeting today about next week, and we won't use it before then.

Yeah, there were a lot of words they objected to — MUFFLER, LUBRICATION, TRIM—part of this program was to come up with these non-sexist, non-violent terminologies for doing

auto repairs. So they also wanted to get rid of words like CHOKE, THROTTLE, BELT, BATTERY, BLEEDING brake lines, you know, things that could injure sensitivities.

Well, it's clear this isn't about getting people working, it's about pursuing a pretty narrow political agenda, one that I think most people would think rather bizarre. You just don't rewrite the language because of a political point of view. Well that's too bad. When you releasing this?

It's part of an ongoing article we're doing for the weekend edition, maybe held to next week depending.

Okay, well we'll wait until you're done using it. Whatever you guys want. If you want to delay giving it to us, that's fine, but whenever you're done, obviously, I'd like to have it.

So this is something you can see using in Question Period?

Yeah, but you want to be careful about who uses it . . . [LAUGHS]

Who would you get to use it? Maybe Deb Grey, with her motorcycle backround could take the question?

She could maybe bring her cigar in when she does that. I appreciate you letting me know. The bottom line is, Canadians are willing to help each other find work, we want to do that, we care about each other, but there's mounting evidence that this fund is not at all about creating jobs for Canadians, and it is everything to do with politics and political agendas. This is just another example of that, I don't think anything you've told me shows there's any serious intent for this money to create jobs. It's clearly designed to be spent for other purposes for political reasons. It's not what Canadians were told by this government, and I don't believe that they'll find that acceptable. If it's not value for money, it's political slush.

FRANK PRANKS

FRANK: What we've got here is $250,000 the Bank of Montreal received in grants to retrain workers who lost their old jobs, due to technological changes in the bank industry. It's pretty routine stuff, data processing courses, that kind of thing. But then they've got someone named A. Sten down for training in origami.

Lorne Nystrom (NDP-Regina-Qu'Appelle) In what?

Origami. At least I HOPE that's what it says. It comes to $17,776 and I've been trying on both the government side and the bank side, but nobody knows what it's about.

Hmm.

Have you heard any of the stuff on the banks?

We'd heard rumours that some of the banks had gotten some transitional job funds, but this is the first one that's coming out in black and white, I suppose?

Yeah. This is a quarter of a million.

I think it's absolutely ridiculous to give a bank that's doing extremely well public funds to retrain workers that the banks themselves have laid off. Here are people that have laid off workers and all the big banks are doing that now. They're closing branches and down-sizing as we all know, and here the federal government is providing the money. It doesn't make any sense. I mean, last year — just let me pull out my file here — the bank's profits were $1.38 billion. $1.38 billion. Matthew Barrett in his swansong year picked up around $20-million, mainly in stock options, as president and CEO of the bank.

Wow.

Yeah, Twenty-million in stock options and salary, which is extremely high, and yet they get $250,000 . . .

He got that in his last year? That includes his severance?

Yup. Twenty million bucks, and it's on the public record. And then he's off to Europe with, what is it, Barclay's now? In England, London? So he gets all that cash and here they qualify for a quarter million dollars of what I call corporate welfare from the taxpayer. That's incredible.

You can certainly argue that they've got the resources to handle this themselves.

Oh, absolutely.

Now, origami, is that that thing with placing things, like which way the doors are facing, for energy . . .

I, I think that's what it is. I have to make a couple of phone calls, but I think that's what that is. But here are the banks, that are laying off people, they could have done it slower through attrition, they're doing very well, it's not as if they're in dire straits and they pick up a quarter million dollars to retrain the people they laid off in the first place. It's . . . disgusting, you know?

That's been the reaction so far today.

I mean, everybody knows the federal jobs fund program has been a disaster. We hear about it all the time. But I didn't know they paid money to companies that cut jobs, to big, wealthy corporations that cut jobs.

Yeah, we're only starting to get some of the specifics now. I guess last week, it was all about the billion dollars — or the three billion, and now we're starting to get some of the specifics.

Well, that's incredible. I haven't seen a minister handle things as badly as this since probably John Fraser on the tuna scandal back in 1985, and it seems to me that she's known about it now for probably several months and didn't come clean on it. It's amazing that a

Ottawa Citizen

David Frum, Page B8

Hollinger denies NDP allegation it accepted grant

BY STEWART BELL

The NDP issued a news release yesterday claiming the federal government had given almost $40,000 to Hollinger, Canada's leading newspaper company, to send a senior executive to the "Cleese Institute of Heraldry" in England.

The allegation was branded "nonsense" by Hollinger, owner

government in a highly evolved country where public administration has been around for a long time and accountability, with auditor generals and so on, would allow this kind of thing to happen. I think it also shows the — I'm sorry to ramble, but —

Oh, no, that's —

We're in so dire need of proper reform in this country so that decision-makers are accountable. Liberal backbenchers are nothing but eunuchs, you know? You read about this in the paper, uh, we have no real accountability, no independence in parliamentary committees. If we had parliamentary committees with any sense of independence — you know, the committees could call witnesses and cross-examine people and timetable legislation and launch their own investigations —

Have your people been trying to get some specifics of where the money's gone?

My understanding is yes, that they've been trying to do that through the research office in Ottawa.

Yeah. the one that's been the most interesting for us is Hollinger got $40,000.

Conrad!

Yep.

Heh-heh. What did he get that for?

They sent one of their vice-presidents to England to take a course in heraldry at the Cleese Institute in London. Now aside from the idiotic waste of money, the *Post* has been quite aggressive on this job creation fund and then on the other hand is taking their shilling, and again, no followup documentation.

Was this when they thought Conrad would become Sir Conrad in the House of Lords?

Well, um, it's before that, but that's a good point. This one's dated '98, the application...

Interesting timing on that. Because it was shortly after that, it was about a year or so ago that kerfuffle took place where Chretien was saying "no." Remember that?

Mm-hm.

And the lobbying was going on and the British were obviously saying "yes."

It seems to be a fairly clear case of hypocrisy here. I'm still waiting for my calls back from Mr. Black, but I'm not holding my breath.

This is absolutely scandalous and people deserve a very independent inquiry as to what the hell's going on and also the RCMP should be involved in this as well.

Is that what's on the agenda in the House next week?

I'm sure it is. I'm sure it is. This'll be the issue and I'm sure it's going to be almost the exclusive issue in the House.

Well, thank you very much, Mr. Nystrom, I'll keep you posted as —

Heraldry, eh?

Yeah.

What would this exactly involve?

Like most of these applications, it doesn't say. It's at the Cleese Institute and um . . . $40,000 to send a vice president . . . Well, it's $39,906 to be fair.

Okay, let me write that down. $39,906. To send one of their vice-presidents?

Yeah.

Of Hollinger, right?

Yes.

To England?

To England.

To take a course on heraldry?

Introductory heraldry.

Ohhhh. Do you have a copy of that particular one you could fax me?

I, uh, I do. What's your fax number there?

I wouldn't mind having some fun with the *National Post*. I'm actually a bit partisan to your paper. More than a bit and I wouldn't mind having some fun with this. That number is 306-359-7353.

Mm-hm. So, VP of Hollinger . . . I'd love a copy of that.

Absolutely. I'll try and get that to you today, but definitely tomorrow.

Thanks a million.

No problem.

Yeah, and the bank stuff, it's just bloody ridiculous.

Well, I can send along a copy of that if you're interested as well.

Okay, yeah, bank stuff I am, I love all the banking stuff. And also the Hollinger. Great stuff!

FRANK PRANKS

FRANK: Calling to get your reaction to some ATI documents concerning a business in your riding, Big Red's, it's a strip club that received...

Randy White (Ref-Langley-Abbotsford): A strip club!?

Are you aware of it?

No.

It received $15,000 in 1998. The documents say the money was to pay for "dance classes for the ladies" and to offset the cost of the establishment's 99 cent Spaghetti dinners for the poor...

A strip place in my riding? Are you sure? That would be very unusual. We're d'ya say it was?

The documents are a bit blurry, but it looks like the place is just off the Trans-Canada somewhere.

Do you got a minute? It doesn't sound like Langley-Abbotsford. [GOES OFF TO GET A PHONE BOOK].

The club's owned by a well known Liberal called Sam Giancana. What you know about him?

Oh, that's gotta be Vancouver.

Do you know Mr. Giancana?

I think he's a Vancouver ... his name comes up regularly ... Just a sec ... [GOES TO GET ANOTHER PHONE BOOK] ... Big Reds ... Clubs, I guess it is ... I understand Mr. Giancana is some kind of wheeler-dealer in Vancouver-Surrey or somewhere. I don't know much about him, but the name's familiar.

Do you think he's spreading his operations further east?

When was this? In 1998? You can get a lot of clubs around here, but a strip club?

Maybe it was some kind of fly-by-night operation?

If it's in Langley-Abbotsford, I would suggest to you that it's under a false name. You may have more there than you think.

It's like when you tell someone just to have one drag on a marijuana joint...

What's your initial reaction to hearing this?

I'd be amazed that it would even be in this area, but I guess anything goes.

Yeah, some critics I've talked to, including women's groups, have argued that while it may be feeding the poor, it's promoting loose morals and leading to the over-sexing of the homeless ...

Oh yeah, I'm gonna have a lot to say about it, but I'm not sure you're on the right track ...

What, you don't have a homeless problem in Langley?

No, I think that's Vancouver. But I agree with the comments, but this sounds like a big thing.

I guess you've never visited Big Red's?

Oh God, no. No!

Since I've got you on the line, maybe I can ask you about another grant I've been hearing about.

Sure.

This was for $25,000 grant to a computer club called Kids.com in Brantford, Ont. — say, isn't that Jane Stewart's riding — where 12 teenagers spent last summer learning all about online stock trading. There's some followup documentation here, but the

kids lost all the money in three days and spend the rest of the summer on welfare ...

[SIGHS] Yeah. Well, it's the same thing out of this whole fund. We knew that basically, no-one is managing this. The shame of it all is that it's just money down the tube in many cases. And the people who are worse off aren't just the taxpayer, it's the people who are involved in these projects that think there's something at the end of it for them, only to find out that it was longtime pain for shortime gain. That's the sad part of it.

What's your reaction, on the moral side of encouraging underage kids to gamble, and over-stimulating homeless men with strip clubs?

This is part of the problem. It's the immorality, where they don't differentiate between the right and wrong of giving money with no end result. And there's no discretion about who you give the money to or why. The immoral part is the young people with expectations, the teaching young people with different moral value content, the whole topic in and of itself hasn't been looked at. Just looking at the phone book, Big Red's not even in the Vancouver phone book.

Well the ATI documents definitely say Langley. Maybe it went out of business.

I'm gonna follow it up. I'll find it for you. Sure. Big Red's in Langley. You might be onto something bigger than you think. The name kind of rings a bell, and that might have been a scam.

What do you think the larger impact of programs like this is on young kids?

The whole methodology is really teaching you that there's free money out there to spend on frivolous things. So all you have to do is ask for money for the stupidest thing and you get it, therefore, why can't

I have money for anything I want without evaluating whether it's necessary, moral, whether it has a future benefit to our society. Teaching responsibility to those who apply for it isn't even a part of the venue.

Is it too far of a stretch to think that these kids are going to sap the system further down the road. If they get hooked on gambling, what kind of burden on society will they be?

It's like when you tell someone just to have one drag on a marijuana joint. I mean where do you go from there?

So you see these programs as a bit of a gateway drug?

If that's what you're gonna start teaching them, you can expect if they're successful at it, in a game or so, they'll pursue it. Like, so, you're really encouraging something that parents wouldn't likely encourage. Their goal is to teach them that dependency on government money is a good thing.

Yeah, if they spend the money in three days, we don't even know the cost of these kids being on welfare for the rest of the summer.

Yeah that plus the expectation, you know, I've got money now, I'm satisfied now, I can go spend it now, and gee, if I don't have a job at the end of it, I can go ask for some more. If I can't get it through a grant like that, well that welfare system is there. It's the values system they're teaching that's inappropriate. I'm gonna get to the bottom of this, cause I think you're onto something that's bordering on a scam.

FRANK: I just received some documents concerning HRDC grants.

Jake Hoeppner (Ref-Portage-Lisgar): Well I haven't seen the documents, but what I can say is that I think it's just a real plus for Canadians that these manipulations, or corruptions, will become public so they can deal with them.

One of the documents I received was to hire a part-time chicken wrangler— or maybe that's strangler, I'm reading from a blurry photocopy here . . .

No that would be a wrangler probably, catching chickens when they're moved around the barns.

Right. It went to the the Wacumba Haitian Voodoo congregation in Shawinigan, I guess that's the Prime Minister's riding. I didn't know this but apparently there's a small Haitian community in . . .

. . . In the agriculture industry . . .

I guess, it's been there since 1926. But there's no listing for such a church, or whatever it is — at least not in English anyway. Maybe there's something in French, or Haitian patois. But what do you think about this?

I wish farmers would get that kind of money to be farmers. I have a lot of farmers in a deficit for the last several years and then to see that...it doesn't create a lot of public trust in

You know I've heard it mentioned, voodoo, but I don't know what it is or what it does to me.

government.

I know this is a rather delicate issue when you're dealing with religion, but voodoo, that isn't an official religion is it?

I don't know what it is. Voodoo sounds more like a cult to me. I don't think government should be funding any religious organization. We are there to run the public purse and to do what is right for the average taxpayer.

What kind of concerns do you have about taxpayers money supporting a cult?

I think they should have the freedom to organize and practice their cult, or whatever it is, but surely it shouldn't be at the taxpayers' expense.

You don't know any Haitian voodoo congregations in your neighbourhood do you?

Oh, no, I don't think we have any of them in my riding, maybe in Winnipeg somewhere, that's about the closest you'd come to finding people who belong to the Haitian congregation or culture.

So no voodoo practitioners near you?

No, I've never heard of it, you know I've heard it mentioned, voodoo, but I don't know what it is or what it does to me. It sounds like a cult when I read the things are happening.

Yeah, from what I know about it, it's based on animalistic and human sacrifice . . .

Oh, is that right? Well, that's something makes my stomach growl.

Would you have a concern with the Prime Minister directing money toward a constituent like that?

He has to be held accountable to that. And once the House resumes there will be a lot of questions to him on this issue. I'm sure there has been a lot of research done by the different parties. If you have it, I'm sure they have it too.

FRANK PRANKS

 Jack Ramsay (Ref-Crowfoot): Sorry for getting back to you so late, but I called with the off chance that you'd still be working on this boondoggle of Jane Stewart's.

FRANK: The reason I'm calling is that I've received some ATI documents concerning a job creation program in Halifax called StreetSmarts, which got $98,000 and change to hire four people to set up a website for the homeless people called StreetWise. The idea was to provide information on weather, locations for hot air grates, meal times and menus at various soup kitchens, vacancy rates at hostels, how to get around anti-panhandling laws in Ontario, that kind of thing. It also had an email system so street people can communicate with each other. While it sounds pretty worthwhile, it didn't quite work out . . .

What d'ya mean not work out?

It involved loaning 20 laptops to various people on the street . . .

On the street!?

As you can imagine, they didn't last very long.

Aww.

Within two weeks, 18 were reported stolen. One of they guys who stole one — you might have read this in the papers — was arrested for sending lewd and threatening emails to Ashley MacIssac, and the last guy, unfortunately, froze to death while using his.

I think that the homeless problem needs to be addressed, but this isn't the right way to do it. If we think we can solve the homeless problem by giving people a laptop, to find out where there's a hot air grate, I don't think that's the answer. The fundamental cause of unemployment has been created by our high rate of taxation which is taking so much money out of the pockets of the individuals, our families, the strength of our community is based on the strength of the family. And surely if families are economically strong, they will not allow their family members to survive on a hot air grate. But when they're taking 50-55 cents of every dollar you earn, how can you do anything other than keep your own immediate family household together? The idea of taxing us to death and then thinking a laptop in the hands of street person is the answer to his problem, is nonsense. They should have seen the failure of it before they even began.

> They know where to get the crack, where they can get the marijuana, where they can get the booze.

It had other problems to, the computer guys who set up the project billed $5,008.79, for pizza, subs and soft drinks. . . .

Aww, on and on it goes.

There's a larger issue involved here as well. Some of the people using these computers had been accessing inappropriate websites. I mean these are Mac, G-3s. Very high-tech, with remote Internet access, the whole nine yards, and these guys were watching pornography. . . .

Of course, you have to always assess where the street person is at and how best to help them. If you're going to simply give them cash, you have to count on them spending it in a way that's positive. But what if they're not motivated to do that. Then what you do?

What kind of concerns do you have about the taxpayer subsidizing a homeless guy's porn addiction?

Aww. The question is how is that helping them, how is that alleviating what the government perceives as a problem? Obviously, the government perceives the homeless person's problem different than the homeless person perceives it. And that's the problem. So they have a $3000 computer they can sell off or sit there and watch pornographic information. So, over to you Mr. Government, how do you explain this? So it looks good on paper, that these people are going to be able to access where there's a grate, where there's a homeless shelter or whatever. That sounds wonderful. Those people know where the grates are. The know where the food. They know where the shelters are.

And where the porn is, too.

Absolutely. Absolutely. And they know where to get the crack, where they can get the marijuana, where they can get the booze. They know all of this. They're spending all their money on booze and drugs, and they're getting their room and board for free, paid for by the taxpayer. They're making their $100 a day, they got no worries, they got no responsibilities, they like the lifestyle. What is the government going to do?

Some of these grants are handed out quite liberally. Another one in Ontario, called Squeegee Clean in downtown Toronto got $26,808. Looking at the paperwork here, it was a training course to get street kids into the squeegee business. Its learning modules included Proper Squeegee Techniques, Traffic Safety, Squeegee Fashion, Legal Issues, like girls going topless, Tax Liabilities, Investing Tips, that kind of thing. Don't you think it's a little weird that the federal government is supporting something at the same time as the Ontario government is outlawing it?

They're out of touch. No question. First the homeless, and now this. It speaks again for them to get with the people they are attempting to assist.

What's your initial reaction to topless squeegee kids?

Ah, er...All you gotta do is talk to some of the people approached by these kids, we don't have them in my town, where you're gonna be approached in that way. Talk to the people they're trying to serve. I think the Government of Ontario has been hearing from those people and that's why they're moving in the opposite direction. Who in the world set up a program to teach squeegee kids? I've never heard of that. How they know what is a proper and ethical way to approach a car stopped at a stop light? Who designed the program, and from whence does it come from?

You don't think the Liberal government, being as left wing as it is, is paving the way for outdoor strippers with this kind of funding, do you?

If you ask the people, you'll get your answer. Ask anyone driving down the street whether they want that kind of approach. We've got windshield wipers for God's sake and it carries a gallon of . . . of . . . of . . . whuff, you know, of washer fluid.

Do you think it would be fair to say this is just the thin end of the wedge, that in a few years we'll see a program like this for prostitution?

[SIGH] All I can say is that it's not

going to work, I don't think the people will stand for it, I don't think they want it, and they don't want their tax dollars paying for it. Where's the end to all of this, particularly when you have a department that's handing out millions of dollars without any applications, or any trace of where it's going or who's getting it.

 FRANK: I was wondering whether you had heard anything about a program in Pierre Pettigrew's own riding, at least I think so, it's on rue St. Denis in downtown Montreal. It's called L'École de lutte professionelle Mad Dog — I guess that means . . .

Jean Dube (PC-Madawaska-Restigouche): Mad Dog Vachon . . .

> Boy, you've got some good information.

Dube

Maybe it's named after him. According to documents, it got $122,500 . . . **$122,500!**

. . . to provide makeup training, costume design, and character development courses for wannabee professional wrestlers. It got a second grant for $39,875 to hire a part-time speech teacher to help francophone

wrestlers get rid of their French accents or anglophone wrestlers to work on their French accents, depending of course, on what kind of character they'd adopt. **Okay.**

There's no follow-up documentation on this one, and it's over $160,000.

This is the first I've heard of L'École de lutte Vachon. Now that you've brought it to my attention I'm certainly going to take a look and see what's at stake here. Have any jobs been created here?

One for the speech therapist, and the application says about another 10 would be on staff. But there's no documentation as to whether they did. **Boy, you've got some good information. You got lucky like I did last week. I'll check it out and get back to you.**

 FRANK: One of the documents I received was for a $6,500 grant to a chicken wrangler, or is that chicken strangler? The photocopy here is kinda blurry...

Jim Pankiw (Ref-Saskatoon-Humboldt): [LAUGHS].

> I'm at a loss of words. There's a Latin expression, whatsit, "It speaks for itself"?

Pankiw

FRANK PRANKS

. . . it went to the Wacumba Haitian voodoo congregation in Shawingan. I didn't know this but supposedly there's some kind of Haitian community there . . .

You've got to be kidding. Just when you thought it couldn't possibly get any worse.

I called there and there's no listing for any such Church, at least not in English. Maybe in French or Haitian patois. But what's your reaction to money going to a project like that?

Well that's insulting to every taxpayer in the country. It's a national disgrace. If that actually ended up in the Prime Minister's own riding, then he should resign. There's no question the present and former ministers should resign. That's without question. But if this is reaching into the PM's own riding. . . . Did he sign off on it? We deserve an explanation. I'm at a loss of words. There's a Latin expression, whatsit, "It speaks for itself"?

It's been a while since I took Latin class. Are you surprised to hear there's a Haitian community in Shawinigan?

I don't know. I'm a Canadian and look at everybody as a Canadian. I'm really opposed to multiculturalism and to affirmative action quotas, employment equity programs, yadda yadda.

I know this is a rather delicate question considering it deals with religion, but from what I understand about voodooism is that it involves occasional animal and human sacrifice. What kind of concerns do you have around that?

I don't know anything about that. Who got the money again?

The Wacumba Haitian Voodoo Congregation, but when I tried tracking down this organization to get some answers, I couldn't find any such organization. But it's gone somewhere into Chretien's riding . . . You don't have any such congregations in your riding in Saskatoon, do you?

Things like what? I guess there's not much to say other than the issue speaks for itself. I don't know, how . . . I'm at a loss of words. That's infuriating, to think that there's that kind of mismanagement at the level of the federal government. And how insulting is that to families who are struggling to make ends meet under the burdens of our tax levels, to know that's where some of the money's going? It's outrageous!

[PANKIW CALL BACK AN HOUR LATER]
Pankiw: Listen, after I got talking to you, I got back to what I was working on and I realized that this is some kind of joke.
FRANK: Really?
Yeah, when you called I was working on a Revenue Canada case, a guy, three kids, and he's facing backruptcy. And you catch a guy off guard with this thing and you distract the train of thought of a guy who's working on something like that . . . I guess what I'm trying to say is, why don't you go and get job as a real journalist. Like, you know, wouldn't you sooner have a job with real integrity? Does it make you feel good to interrupt me, and I'm not trying to be confrontational here, I'm just thinking here, I'm a member of parliament trying to help a guy facing bankruptcy, I always take calls from journalists and call right them right back. Like . . . I just wanted to offer that suggestion to you. To know what I'm doing, that when you called I was doing some good honest work trying to help somebody . . . [sounding unstable and shrill]. . . . I'm just trying to offer you a suggestion, I think you probably have some good journalistic ability, you should go get a job with a paper.

FRANK: One grant for $22,000 went to the "Lucky" Minh Live Bait Co. to hire an earthworm-sexer for the April-September fishing season in 1998 . . .

John Reynolds (Ref-West Vancouver-Sunshine Coast): An earthworm what?

Sexer.

I'm absolutely astounded. I don't dispute that grants are given, but when there's no follow-up to make sure the money has been spent properly . . . but some of these sound like political payoffs.

Coming from Vancouver, you haven't heard of any companies in your riding who have received similar grants for earthworm-sexers?

I have a hard time getting them for legitimate reasons. When you see programs about, geez, some worms or something, I don't think the Canadian public will understand it. But I think the whole thing is about political interference. The staff hands out grant money without doing proper checks. It's political payola.

When you see programs about, geez, some worms or something

Reynolds